Stages of Ages

Rechilding Your Inner Child

"It's never too late to have a happy childhood"
S. Landsman

by

Elaine Childs Gowell, PhD and Sharon Glantz

authorHOUSE™

1663 LIBERTY DRIVE, SUITE 200
BLOOMINGTON, INDIANA 47403
(800) 839-8640
WWW.AUTHORHOUSE.COM

First published by AuthorHouse 4/11/2006

ISBN: 1-4208-7438-1 (sc)

Library of Congress Control Number: 2005906809
Printed in the United States of America
Bloomington, Indiana

This book is printed on acid-free paper.

ACKNOWLEDGEMENTS

The Corrective Parenting/Rechilding model was born from the efforts of a number of innovative therapists and their clients. Pam Levin, R.N. Clinical Member ITAA, identifies six stages of development through which human beings grow to reach adulthood and has described them in her book <u>Cycles of Power</u>. A seventh stage, the prenatal stage has been the work of Sandra Landsman, Ph.D. Clinical Member ITAA, in <u>Found, a Place for Me</u> and <u>I'm Special</u>. Jean Clarke, Ph.D., made this developmental model accessible to the public through her parenting <u>handbook Self-Esteem a Family Affair</u>. Jacqui Schiff, MSW, can be credited for the development of the Reparenting Model used at the Cathexis Institute. The Cathexis Reader and All My Children were books written about the work at Cathexis Institute. Many of the procedures used in Reparenting were written about by Elaine Childs-Gowell, ARNP, Ph.D. Clinical Member ITAA, in her books <u>Reparenting Schizophrenics: The Cathexis Experience</u>, <u>Bodyscript Blockbusting</u>, and the <u>Cathexis Primer</u>. These procedures have since been called "healing rituals". Elaine coined the word "Rechilding" to describe the other part of the Corrective Parenting coin. Brenda Schaeffer coined the word "Corrective Parenting" with the publication of the developmental chart by that name.

Contents

INTRODUCTION to PART I

By ELAINE CHILDS-GOWELL. ARNP. PHD.

CONTRACTION CORRECTIVE PARENTING AND RECHILDING

I have been thinking about the therapeutic process that is offered through Corrective Parenting Therapy. When I was participating in this process for my own personal growth, I needed to heal the frightened and traumatized child who lived within me. As the adult child of dysfunctional parents, I needed someone who could offer me a strong "healthy parent" from which to model one of my own. This healthy parent had to have the power to protect my frightened child and be also powerful enough to give me permission to find health. The healthy parent I selected had to be more powerful than my own archaic and dysfunctional parent. The therapist who would model my new healthy parent had to be able to provide protection for me from my old internal dysfunctional parent who often sought to abuse me. I needed someone who would take care of my own archaic parent's sick child parts (the child within the archaic parent, within me) and who could give me permission to LIVE, to BE, to DO, to THINK, and to FEEL, to BE who I really am and to have my own power, to succeed in life. This permission had to be powerful enough so that I could explore all the old unfinished, and painful pieces of archaic business that were still blocking my ability to live my life as fully as I was entitled to as a whole human being. I needed to be fully bonded with me, loving myself and interdependent with others, instead of filled with self-hatred and fear of commitment to life to others. Bonding is probably the most important thing in human and mammal life and yet parents are puzzled because they "give their chil-

1

dren everything", except the deep spiritual bond that is most needed by all of us, and then wonder why "things went wrong." I had to bond with my therapist before I could examine what went wrong. From there I was able to bond with myself and love myself unconditionally.

The bonding process took me through the steps of checking out whether the therapist was "competent" to model a healthy parent for my Child. For some people this checking-out and trusting process takes a fairly long time. Some clients never complete the healthy transference that they need to be able to successfully carry through with their therapeutic experience, all the way to health and happiness. For me, my choice of therapists was unerring, and I was fortunate to have a therapist for each part of my process who facilitated my healing at each step of my way. Their contracts with me were, in essence: "I will be a Healthy Parent for your Child". "I will take care of your Child, under contract, no matter what". "I will take care of your archaic parent's child so you can be free to be a healthy child your self and so you can experience a healthy childhood."

The process of Corrective Parenting therapy starts with a general Life Script Interview (Holloway 1975) and a Developmental Life Script Questionnaire (Levin 1982). These are powerful tools which assisted me to acknowledge that my family was truly dysfunctional in ways that had impacted me adversely. I had to take responsibility for the changes I needed to make in my own self in order to be able to get past the denial, and the belief that my family was "normal". As a therapist I have my client review his/her life goals and he/she and I go over and agree to a series of contracts aimed at accomplishing these life goals. These contracts are both short-term, and long-term contracts. They are underwritten theoretically by the therapeutic intervention known as "closing loopholes" (Holloway 1974; Boyd and Boyd 1979; Boyd 1986). What this process did for me in my own growth was that this helped set up protection from the "escape hatches" I had devised for my Desperate Child. It is not unusual for abused and battered children to vow to themselves that if "things get too bad, I can always . . . run away, kill myself, get sick etc., and then they'll be sorry and stop abusing me". These vows often become a part of the subconscious motivation for dealing with life as a grown-up.

SELF CARE CONTRACTS

The self-care contracts speak to the part of the person who made the vow, i.e. the defense/survival system. They make it clear that this therapy is serious and safe and that the therapist really cares is truly powerful (i.e. more powerful than the crazy parts of one's own personality) and really means business. My clients and I have found these contracts to be a most powerful tool in guiding us to achieve our goals in life. In many ways the contracts provide the same level of personal power that the Twelve Steps do, only in a different way. The self-care contracts address the underlying dysfunctional issues in the personality structure. When I had difficulty keeping any one of these contracts, I became aware of what the script issues were which were generating the contract-breaking behavior and that needed to be worked on and cleared up. Often when I broke any one of these contracts I would have "thinking time out" so that I could figure out what the therapeutic issues were and which Corrective Parenting or other therapeutic intervention was needed in order for me to make the necessary changes on the psychological level. We have a procedure called the "accountability work" or the "think chair" which is followed for this purpose.

The first of the SELF CARE contracts is I WILL NOT KILL MY-SELF ACCIDENTALLY OR ON PURPOSE, NOR WILL I CON-TRIBUTE TO MY DYING (Boyd 1986), I WILL BE HEALTHY AND RESPONSIBLE. This agreement addresses the existential issues, which many of us face. We have found that if the client has pre- and peri-natal and/or early childhood issues this contract will stir these up and then the issues will more easily be seen and worked on. It was important to me because through it I discovered the part of me that was angry at my mother not lactating and feeding me when I was a newborn, and had decided to get even with her.

I WILL NOT HARM MYSELF, NOR WILL I PROVOKE OTH-ERS TO HARM ME; I WILL RESPECT OTHERS AND MYSELF AND ACT IN A RESPONSIBLE WAY. This one helped me face up to some of the harmful habits I had developed, particularly some of the compulsive and co-dependent behaviors I had chosen as a part of my life script.

I WILL NOT GET SICK OR GO CRAZY; INSTEAD, I WILL BE-COME SANE AND HEALTHY AND WORK THROUGH PROB-LEMS RESPONSIBLY BY STRUCTURING MY WORK WITHIN A CONTRACT.   As a child and later as an adult I did not have per-mission to express my feelings freely or appropriately. I would store things up until I couldn't stand it, and then I would blow up. I did not believe that I could get my needs met in appropriate ways and I used sickness and crazy acting-out behaviors to express myself, to try to get some of my needs met.

This contract created a climate in which I could start facing some of the issues I had around getting my needs met and expressing my thoughts and feelings appropriately.

I WILL NOT RUN AWAY PHYSICALLY OR PSYCHOLOGI-CALLY; I WILL STAY, WORK THROUGH MY FEELINGS, THOUGHTS AND BEHAVIOR AND SOLVE PROBLEMS. This was very important to me as it got me to focus on the ways in which I could avoid doing what needed to be done in my therapeutic process. The habits of script are so strong that it was easy to side step or run from or slip by some important issues. Besides, I was into being a "workaholic", and working hard was a good way to run away. Running away had served me well for most of my life until I started living by the self-care contracts. Running away had saved me from many a beating, for, when I came back, sometimes my mother had forgotten that she was mad at me and I would escape another thrashing punishment. The contract helped me be aware of all of the other slick and sneaky ways I had of running away, and it was supported by the next one.

I WILL NOT BE SNEAKY OR LIE; I WILL BE HONEST WITH MYSELF AND OTHERS BOTH INTELLECTUALLY AND EMO-TIONALLY. This means that I will be honest about my thoughts and feelings and not sneak or fudge or twist the truth in order to get by, as I had to do in my family of origin. This contract was also important to me in that it forced me to recognize the ways in which I was not honest with myself and others; how defensive I would get to cover up my scare at being "found out."

I WILL NOT BE PASSIVE, I WILL BE REACTIVE TO MY OWN AND OTHER THOUGHTS, FEELINGS, AND BEHAV-IORS. This contract assists me to share my thoughts and feelings openly and honestly and helps me deal with what is going on right now. It makes it impossible to redefine, to remain silent and to ignore whatever may be going on in the present. It reinforces personal accountability. It is the basic contract for everything I do in my life, as a therapist, as a friend, as a human being. It is the basic contract underlying the whole therapeutic process, which is called Corrective Parenting. This contract supports all of the other contracts, which are made as a part of the Corrective Parenting process. I often think about how fortunate I am to have been guided through this process by my therapists and teachers in the Transactional Analysis field. I have been involved for the past 30 years in creating a community of therapists and clients who can also benefit as I have from this process.

The Corrective Parenting and Rechilding rituals are the result of a dialog between therapists and clients involved in this process. These healing rituals embody the tools and procedures by which persons can challenge their dysfunctional and co-dependent behaviors and become healthy functioning adults. It's really true! IT'S NEVER TOO LATE TO HAVE A HAPPY CHILDHOOD.

As you read this book, please keep an open mind. Much of the material may seem bizarre and very much out-of-the-ordinary, indeed, extra-ordinary. This book has come out of the actual experiences of many hundreds of people over thirty years, and that is a true account of what happened to them. Read it with courage, and with the knowledge that it is supported by research and the actual experiences of many people, including myself.

PART I.
MODELS, OLD AND NEW

They behaved themselves. Time had passed since their move to the new pool. The zookeepers assumed the otters were settled into their new home. But were they? Why weren't the otters playing? Otters are known for their playfulness. Yet, here in their new environment they did not play. And thus they were when Gregory Bateson, noted for his research in systems analysis, paid them a visit. Bateson observed the otters, reflecting on their estranged behavior. Why weren't they playing? He tied a piece of paper to a string and dropped it over the edge of the pool. The first otter reached out and pawed the piece of paper. Soon another joined in until, once again the otters played in the joyful way they had always played all of their lives.

What had happened to them?

Bateson concluded that they had been stuck in a "playless paradigm, "paradigm" is a pattern, example or model. In the new pool, the otters' view of their world did not include play. However, the piece of paper on the string offered a change of view. Because of the piece of paper, their worldview changed and they were able to break out of the old paradigm.

Like otters, those of us humans who are stuck in old unworkable models must have something different happen in order to change and break from our old ways of operating. With change comes the shift from the old paradigm to the new paradigm – from a negative to a more positive way of being.

How do we accomplish a paradigm shift?

We humans have devised myriad rituals and metaphors throughout history to accomplish paradigm shifts. Rituals and metaphors work within cultural expressions such as religion, rock music, dancing, family gatherings, and psychotherapy.

Rituals make possible a change in our perception of our world. Metaphors help to define and give scope to that change. Together they provide the new or differing perspective we need to more clearly understand where we are stuck.

Modern psychotherapy offers a wide array of healing rituals and metaphors to help people who choose to invest themselves in working towards healthier and happier lives. Lying on a couch, beating a pillow, or dramatizing a traumatic event are examples of healing rituals. Healing rituals and metaphors offer us opportunities to change.

CHANGING PARADIGMS: CORRECTIVE PARENTING

One key feature distinguishes the Corrective Parenting model from other types of psychotherapy; the role of the therapist as a "healthy parent" under contract to the client. Transference is a phenomenon well recognized in modern psychotherapy in which the client subconsciously adopts the psychiatrist or therapist as a parent, attributing to him both the negative and the positive qualities the client expects from a parent. Corrective parenting formalizes the role of the therapist as a healthy "new parent", and helps the client separate and release negative expectations about parents. The parent/child contract creates safety and stimulus for the client's regressive experiences, the focus of the Corrective Parenting process. As a healthy "new" parent, the therapist supports the client in regressing for the time-limited pieces of work to any age from conception on. The "mom" or "dad" interacts with the contracted "child" in ways appropriate to a parental relationship with an actual child. These interactions are the basic rituals of the model. For instance, activities included holding, feeding with a bottle, lovingly restraining a one-year-old from pulling a load over, and answering questions about sexuality for a four-year-old.

In addition to the corrective rituals of the model, the therapist also supports the client in rituals designed intensify the original unhealthy experiences in order to bring these into full consciousness and set the stage for the Corrective Parenting rituals. These rites of intensification include exercises for anger and fear, sadness and joy, such as laughing raucously, pulling a towel and struggling while being restrained. Clients learn about these and many other commonly used rituals. They are also encouraged to devise new rituals tailored to suit their individual needs. Through both types of ritual, the therapist and client work together to diminish the power of early destructive and abusive parent messages and replace them with a new set of appropriate and supportive parent messages about self-esteem, self-care, values and limits. Eventually the client internalizes the role of the new parent and assumes the healthy parenting role within him.

Unhealthy Parent Messages Create Paradigms that do not Work

Those of us who incorporated unhealthy parenting about ourselves continue to parent ourselves in unhealthy ways. We then do not take care of ourselves appropriately, not eating as we should, not resting as we should, and not enjoying our lives as is our birth right. We tend to experience life as painful, and resort to self-medicating in a variety of dysfunctional ways, from using alcohol and drugs to using food, work, sex, and a myriad of other means to deaden our pain.

Where do these unhealthy parent messages come from?

From parents. From the parents of our parents. From the parents of the parents of our parents and so on. Many old parent messages relate to the peculiar value systems, experiences and self-esteem levels of our parents and their parents; other relate to cultural values and norms. These messages may condition views about scarcity, sex, money, prosperity, food, religious beliefs and political opinions. They may have served the culture protecting standards and ways of co-existing that are no longer useful in this day and age. Some of them may also have become hazardous to the individual who tries to abide by them.

- No talking at the table!

- Sex is ---- shshshshsh!

- You must struggle to get what you want.

- You don't really want that.

- I wish that you were never born.

We absorb these messages with the most primitive parts of the brain and body. If we experience physical abuse, the negative messages are even more deeply imprinted. Our conscious awareness of the messages is not enough to protect ourselves from them.

How do we know which negative messages we've actually internalized?

Voice tones, body language, and defense structures demonstrate gaps in development that interfere with healthy adult living. We live out these gaps in our adult relationships, work and play. Corrective Parenting supports the client in identifying the developmental gaps and provides a safe environment, healthy new parents and ritual tools for correcting the gaps.

INTRODUCTION TO PART II

By ELAINE CHILDS-GOWELL. ARNP. PHD.

IT'S NEVER TOO LATE TO HAVE A HAPPY CHILDHOOD

The template or pattern for much of the anguish and pain experienced in adult life is set in the pre and perinatal periods, as well as the early months of life. The fetus' and the baby's nervous systems record the traumas, feelings and experience of the mother during her pregnancy as a sort of "cellular memory" (Farrant 1987; Verney 1986). The manner in which the baby is handled at birth and during the weeks soon after has a profound effect on the attitudes, intellect and world view of that person. Research is amassing that supports this view. The mishandling of babies at birth causes the babies to lose nervous tissue in the key parts of the brain such as the Corpus Callosum (cited by Jean Houston at a workshop on 12/9/84). The Corpus Callosum is the large bundle of nerves that connects the right brain hemisphere with the left-brain hemisphere. Research supports the view that people with thinking and feeling disorders have impairment in their ability to connect their sensory input with their thoughts and feelings. They demonstrate definite malfunction of the limbic system. The Leboyer babies and the "water babies" which are being followed in the research are showing that babies who have a careful and tender introduction to the world are happier, more intelligent, better adjusted and more psychic, and more in tune with their world than found in the general public.

Modern obstetrical practices have been causing untold damage to babies, and may be one of the factors in the violence in our society. Babies who have been violated will carry the violation in their nervous systems and will seek to re-enact it at some later time in their lives, causing themselves and others considerable pain. (Grof, 1988). Most of psychotherapy is the Grief Process. We are grieving the pain of past assaults on our system. Many hundreds of clients of Corrective Parenting have found that challenging the abusive and violating experiences they had as infants, babies, and children, can actually change the set of their nervous systems. They can move away from fight, flight, or freeze, their automatic reactions to conflict to a point where they have personal satisfaction, flexibility, and control. Many do even find a measure of happiness and freedom to <u>Be Who They Are</u>, fully and completely.

PART II
THE CORRECTIVE PARENTING PROCESS

HOW RITUAL AND METAPHOR WORK TOGETHER

Ritual and metaphors work together in the Corrective Parenting process by providing developmentally based experiences which evoke past memories and provoke flashbacks which can serve to release archaic energy and admit new messages thus building new neuronal pathways of experience.

Metaphors are conceptual tools of language that condense meaning. In the Corrective Parenting process metaphors are used to describe the client's developmental gaps and unworkable paradigms, and also tasks and rituals that will help him fill in those gaps. The metaphors provide structure, set limits and boundaries, and engender feelings of safety and security.

> I had the group wrap me up in a sheet. I wanted to feel like I was in my mother's womb. But I couldn't get comfortable. I began to squirm and push against the sheet. "Don't smother me, Mom, don't smother me." I heard myself scream. I remember my mom exerted a great deal of control over me when I was a child. Her doting and overprotecting made me feel like I was being smothered. She didn't want me, I just know it!

Rituals are behavioral tools for manipulating human emotion. Like actors in a drama, the participants move into an altered state where they remain in control while at the same time open to new ways of perceiving new stimuli. In the Corrective Parenting process, rituals give the client and therapist access to the less conscious aspects of the personality. Within the structure provided by the metaphors, the rituals spark creativity, spontaneity and new perspectives and decisions.

> **I felt like I always had to check out how my mom felt about anything before I checked out how I felt about it myself. I felt that I had to protect her from feeling her feelings because I sensed that they were too uncomfortable for her to feel. So I felt them for her. A ritual I developed with my therapist helped me feel separate from her. I made a box into a small room; complete with cushions and other comforts. It was a room I know that my mom would like. My therapist took the picture of my mom I had given her and placed it in the box. She said that my mom was safe and comfortable in her room and that I would not have to take care of her. Each time I came to therapy we would take the picture out of the box and my therapist would remind me that my mom was safe and comfortable in her room and that she was well taken care of. We did all of this with me "being four". I am beginning to really experience that I am truly separate, and that I can feel my own feelings and I do not have to feel my mom's feelings for her. I don't have to "take care" of her!**

The healing process is rarely an easy experience, and it often takes doing some of the rituals over and over. Along the way many clients experience varying degrees of resistance to working in therapy. Resistance is the sign of a model that is not working. It is one of the ways in which we try to sabotage our healthy getting healthier. Resistance can disguise itself as:

- A void of feeling.

- Joking and laughing where there is no humor.

- Projecting onto others denies feelings of anger, sadness or fear.

Resistance turns structure into limitation; framework into rigidity; focus into narrow mindedness. Like the other unworkable models in our lives, resistance is a survival mechanism learned at times in our lives when we needed to find a way to deal with abusive and unhealthy parent messages: one of those messages was the injunction against changing the messages themselves – a message to be resistant.

Clients work through resistance in the same way they work through other unworkable paradigms. They use metaphors and rituals. Throughout the process, the metaphors and rituals work together to facilitate big changes in short intense moments.

THE STAGES OF RITUAL

The three stages of ritual process have been described in the anthropological literature as **SEPARATION, LIMEN, and AGGREGATION.** There is a period of time in preparation for ritual process that separates the participants from their usual ways of being, before they move into the actual experience of the ritual. Limen, or threshold, means participants move through the doorway to an altered state of consciousness. During this time, they are neither of their usual world, nor are they of their world the way it is going to be when they have finished the experiential part of the ritual. The final stage aggregation is where the participants come back into the ordinary world, but now with a new and different status. For example, consider the ritual of marriage which moves the participants from being "single", "unmarried" to being "married" and "coupled", a different status than before the marriage ritual. Each of the stages of a ritual has specific symbols and metaphors that condense the meaning of the stage of the ritual. In psychotherapy rituals, the goal is to assist participants moving from being troubled, depressed, and uncomfortable to a status of serenity and peacefulness about themselves. Rituals of Corrective Parenting follow these three stages.

SEPARATION

Moving into a ritual the client first experiences the feeling of separation from the ordinary and from his/her usual mode of being:

I feel it each time I pass through the doorway into the group therapy room. There is a veil between my day-to-day world

and the one we create as a group during our weekly meeting. The veil is both opaque and translucent depending on the work. The veil wraps protection around us. I recognize how I carry my attachment to that group – that special arena of expression – that surrogate family – as I function within the familiarity of my life. In group, I am safe from the great and petty disturbances of life's maintenance while in touch with the roots of those same disturbances within myself. Unlike my daily existence, here I am conscious of my every gesture, thought, and way of speaking. We're not in Kansas anymore, Toto.

The setting used for this work supports the client's process of separating from the ordinary. Most of the work is done in a group setting either in regular weekly therapy groups or in "marathon" weekend sessions.

The weekly therapy group ranges from 6 to 12 person. I t meets two to four hours and operates under its own norms and rules. Titles, last names, and "making nice" are prohibited. Some behaviors considered normal in the outside world are pointed out as being deceptive, sneaky, defensive, hypocritical or irresponsible. For example, defending someone against someone else's anger or consistently putting off therapeutic work until the end of the group session. Clarity is accomplished through careful confrontation of these behaviors.

Open sharing and confrontation on thoughts and feelings are the order of the sessions. Face-saving defense mechanisms are reacted to immediately by other clients or the therapists(s). Honesty is the only policy. People are expected to practice being totally honest in all of the sessions, whether they are weekly groups or marathon weekend groups.

Marathons operate under the same rules and norms as do groups. They meet for up to 48 hours including time for sleeping, socializing and eating. Eight to twenty clients are attended by two therapists and two to six assistant therapists. Marathons are designed to encompass an entire living experience, providing clients with peer feedback, therapeutic intervention, a place to rehearse the changes they have made, and time to experience new perceptions. Providing a natural gestalt – a unit of learning-time unbroken into bits and pieces – clients experience intensification and acceleration of intimacy and genuine encounter. This is both an organic process and the result of deliberate instigation of the group expectations by the therapists and assistants. Thus the marathon focuses on specific behavioral changes over a set period of time.

Both marathon sessions and weekly group sessions accomplish the stage of separation. Individuals in the group – clients and staff alike – are separated from their daily lives and the routines of the usual and mundane. Confined to the marathon environment or the group space, clients are allowed no outside contact during the sessions, and superficial socializing is discouraged. The work of the marathon or group is based on the contracts made at the beginning. The contracts articulate the work each client plans to do – work they are committed to complete which will bring about the personal changes they have set out to accomplish. It is in this way that the appropriate environment and symbolic behaviors fulfill the first stage of ritual.

LIMEN OR THRESHOLD

After separating from the ordinary, the client moves into the non-ordinary moment defined by the ritual. This is the moment where the client may become aware of decisions and belief systems made at a very young time in his/her life.

> I'm going to feel stupid, I think as I curl into her arms. I'm an adult. No, not while I'm being held like this. How can this be? Be. That's it. That's all. Be. My thought patterns are different. I . . . I don't want to think. I simply want to be here. Be held. Me and my bulk. When held, my body isn't awkward and difficult to deal with. Be me and me and you are me and gaa gaa goo. No clenching over strange behavior – babies don't self-judge. They simply are. I simply am. Rock me, rock me. I'll fidget 'till you rock me. Fidget, squirm, wriggle and writhe. There. You understood. I'm okay. I'm getting what I want. La la la la – thirsty. I could use a nice drink. Fidget, fuss, thirsty. Oh wow! It's my favorites! Apple juice, and a nice nipple. Ah. This is the life. Enough. I said Enough. No! No more! No more bottle! Get it away! Get away! You're always stuffing something into my mouth. You're always making me eat when I don't want anymore. Leave me alone!

Both groups and marathons provide a prototype family as a basis for clients to discover their early traumas and set up new corrective experiences. Clients relate in such a manner so as to increase their awareness of their own parenting skills and the Child within them selves and others. Those who contract to "Be Little" are fed, cared for, played with, etc. according to the age they have contracted to enact.

Every aspect of the developmental cycle may arise for someone sometime during the process. These cycles are experienced and discussed in terms of what the individual can gain from the awareness of what they are experiencing. The developmental issues form the basis for the contracted changes proposed by each person.

INTEGRATION

Finally, in emerging from the working stage of the ritual, the client moves into a time of integrating the experience and brings himself back into the ordinary.

> When I eat, I am loved. The more I eat the more I am loved. I'll eat instead of cry. Will you love me now? I've grown bigger so there's more of me to love and I barely say a word. Will you love me now? I become aware that these questions have rambled through my brain for as long as I can remember. Yes, I've always asked these questions. Whenever mom cooked, I ate. It made her happy. Whenever I wanted to talk and share my life with her, she fed me. Our best times were in the kitchen while she made dinner. Eat to be loved. Feel and get nothing. That was my model. Out it must go. Rather, I know now that I do not have to eat to be loved. I can feel my feelings and still be loved.

Group and marathon sessions both incorporate closing procedures to help clients move out of the therapy setting and re-enter their day-to-day experience. During the check-out the client expresses thought and feeling about the experience during the session, and make their changes concrete by acknowledging how the "work" followed the contracts they made at the beginning of The Ritual Process for closure involves a statement of what was the mistaken belief system or script issue worked on, how it was worked on and the outcome.

These three stages constitute the ritual process. The Corrective Parenting procedures and theory provide a ritual for clients to experience their Child through all of the developmental stages. Each ritual experience provides the client with new metaphors with which he/she can order his/her world.

The Corrective Parenting rituals allow the client to move in and out of an altered state during which the dominant hemisphere of the brain is momentarily distracted.

How does this happen?

Who knows exactly? The shaman, the priestess, the rabbi, the therapist, all receives validation through the changes within the participant as a result of the ritual. However, the "how" remains as yet obscure, yet miraculous. The Corrective Parenting process has been proven helpful to clients in developing their own tools for good health and for appropriate self-care.

INTRODUCTION TO PART III

By A. Sharon Glantz

Until I began my therapy in Corrective Parenting, my participation in the theater was that of a performer and director. As a director, I used ritual, psychodrama-like scenarios and written text, often poetic in form. In developing the courage to originate the play, I continued using this structure. In each piece there are parts where a set of guidelines rather than text is provided for the director and actors to follow. In this way, they develop their own dialog and are encouraged to create their own rituals within parameters required to remain consistent with the concept of the play.

I enjoy using a non-linear format that focuses on a specific issue. I invite actors to bring as much of themselves to the piece as they dare. In this way, the play included scenes of a personal nature with which audiences can more easily empathize and sympathize. The dynamics of the plays grow from the emotional needs around the issue being investigated rather than a plot or story line. They resemble the early mystery and morality plays designed to educate the masses on the virtues and problematic aspects of Christianity. I often draw on the Greeks with their chorus and "deus ex machinas".

As in all theater endeavors, work is done in collaboration with the playwright, director, actors, technicians, producer, requiring a tremendous amount of trust. Presentations reflect not only the quality of the material but the quality of the ensemble as well.

My work in Corrective Parenting helped me include ways of establishing safety and security in order to delve deeply into volatile issues such as AIDS, sexual abuse, etc. I learned how to subtly insert trust-building exercises into the text of my plays to support a strong ensemble as well as a close and interactive relationship with audience members. In directing, I often use contracts as a way of securing cast members' trust in me, trust in each other and trust in themselves.

Because of the incredible time commitment and emotional intimacy required by theater participants in any play, the cast and crew become a family so that with rare exception, everyone's "stuff" surfaces its ugly head at one time or another. The theater process itself with the help of a well-guided director requests the actor to recognize how their personal needs related to the character's needs. Thus, while there is no catharsis, there is a place for the "stuff" as it shows itself.

In preparing Stages of Ages, Elaine and I realized that we needed to present the material about the developmental stages in a different way since Pam Levin' book, Cycles of Becoming does a thorough job. At the same time, I was searching out the theme for my next play. Bringing the therapeutic research of Corrective Parenting and the creative process of drama development together became the obvious next step.

Two productions resulted. The first covered the first 4 stages. The second involved the next 3 stages. Each proved successful both as entertainment and education.

Stages of Ages Part I

HE   Peter Sorenson

SHE   Carolyn Ayres/Mary Lathrop

HIM   G. Valmont Thomas/David Scully

HER   Z. Sharon Glantz

Directing Assistance   Roger Tompkins

[Received BEST OF FESTIVAL honors at New City Theater's Playwrights' Festival in Seattle Washington, January 1988]

Stages of Ages Part II

HE   Mark Rabe

SHE   Mary Lathrop

HIM   Aldrich Allen

HER   Tijuana Layne

Director   Z. Sharon Glantz

[Received BEST OF FESTIVAL honors at the Northwest Playwrights Guild's/Storefront Theater's Playwrights Festival in Portland, Oregon, November 1988]

In each case, the cast members received a sampling of the Corrective Parenting process. All participants felt their experiences in rehearsing the plays resulted in some of the most inventive and creative work they had done. I figured that a scripted and playful regression into early childhood established an environment conducive to letting the imagination reach great heights and great depths.

We made sure we developed the trust required to feel comfortable challenging personal issues around the concepts in the plays. Sometimes we had great difficulty moving through a section. In a few scenes, personal issues took larger focus than what was written. We learned to acknowledge and accept our mutual discomfort, without pushing onto what was behind the discomfort. That would require professional assistance to resolve. We agreed to disagree and did not lose sight of what we were doing. At the forefront of our awareness was the recognition that despite the content, we were producing art – not participating in a therapeutic process.

I support the use of the dialogues and monologues as a part of a healing ritual as well as for fun and entertainment. Use them as a spring board for your own writing or whatever creative process your choose. That's what they're for. If you are inspired to do a full production for a paying audience, respect copyrights and fulfill royalty obligations. I hope you will invite me to celebrate its success either in process of or for its opening.

Theater, whether in process or in production, is a magical ritual unto itself. When I discovered that Corrective Parenting used procedures I recognized as theater games taken a step further, I found healing rituals even more effective. While I am aware of a line that distinguishes art from healing, I know how blurry that line can become in a way that supports both disciplines. Both processes require the participant to move through the 3 stages of ritual and connect with a specific part of themselves. In Corrective Parenting it is the child within. In theater it is those aspects that correlate with the character being portrayed.

Each discipline creates a transformative experience for those involved. For me, bringing the two together doubled the impact. I have witnessed from both an on-stage position as well as from within the audience a great sense of validation and a rise to empowerment by viewers, performers and technicians. Developing a play is like preparing for birth. I am proud to have mothered such strong healthy children. With your participation, they will be nurtured into a healthy adulthood.

PART III.
DEVELOPMENTAL STAGES:
A MODEL FOR CORRECTIVE PARENTING

The Corrective Parenting and Rechilding process works within a model of human development holding that we grow through seven developmental stages to reach adulthood. In each stage we are met with a specific set of tasks that we must accomplish during the months or years that encompass that stage. When we absorb unhealthy parent messages, we may fail to accomplish these tasks, with the result we function in unhealthy ways and live according to unworkable paradigms later in life. Also, unfinished tasks have a tendency to loom larger and larger in our psyches as we grow older making it harder for us to function adequately as grown-ups.

Fortunately, the inclination to accomplish each set of tasks recurs in later stages and throughout adulthood as we re-experience sensations, emotions, needs and urges from the earlier stages. This process, called "recycling", offers opportunities for healing developmental gaps and solidifying healthy growth throughout our lifespan. This outline of the Corrective Parenting developmental model crystallizes and integrates work in progress in a number of Corrective Parenting communities across the United States. Sandy Landsman's material on the prenatal stages in particular is notable. The pre and perinatal process has been further developed through workshops. **Experiencing Enough**, an experiential workshop on prenatal and infant issues, and the **Developmental Stages** workshop.

[THE STAGE IS BARE EXCEPT FOR TWO BLACK BLOCKS AND A COLORFUL CARD-BOARD TOY BOX ALONG SIDE A BOX OF CRAYONS. SHE, HIM AND HER ENTER. THEY EACH WEAR A DIFFERENT BRIGHTLY COLORED MATCHING SET OF SWEATPANTS AND SWEATSHIRTS WITH A HOOD. THEY GREET THE AUDIENCE.]

HE: I'm your average guy.

SHE: I'm a normal person.

HER: Nothing special here.

HIM: I'm like everyone else – like all of you.

HE: I have a mother and a father.

SHE: I have a mother and a father.

HER: I have a mother and a father.

HIM: I have a mother and a father.

HE: I was conceived when –

SHE: my dad impregnated my mom –

HER: and she pushed me through the birth canal –

HIM: so I could grow up.

[THEY PACE ANXIOUSLY]

HE: I grew up with holes in my psyche

SHE: with gaps in my development

HER: with messages I didn't understand

HIM: without acceptance for who I am.

   [THEY CONCUR]

HE: My parents are people.

SHE: My parents are people.

HER: My parents are people.

HIM: My parents are people.

   [THEY JUSTIFY]

HE: They have people problems like your average guy.

SHE: They're not perfect because they are normal.

HER: Nothing special there.

HIM: They are like everyone else—like all of you.

   [THEY CONFRONT]

HE: But their holes became my holes.

SHE: Their gaps are my gaps.

HER: So many things I don't understand.

HIM: It's hereditary – like it is with all of you.

   [THEY DETERMINE]

HE: I wish to fill in the holes for my children and their children.

SHE: I want to fill in the gaps for my sons and daughters.

HER: I will speak with clear messages so my kids will understand.

HIM: I will accept myself and spread acceptance to those I care about.

    [THEY COMMIT]

HE: A search through my history

SHE: a sojourn through my past

HER: a journey back to what happened before

HIM: an exploration of how I became.

ALL: Script rewrite!

    [HE PICKS HIS NOSE. SHE APPROACHES.]

SHE: You shouldn't do that. It's bad for you.

HE: Who's speaking?

SHE: I am.

HE, HIM, HER: Who's speaking?

SHE: My mother.

    [HE POUTS. HER APPROACHES]

HE: I'm no good. I'm worthless.

HER: Who's speaking?

HE: I am.

HER, HE, SHE: Who's speaking?

HE: My father.

> [HER LOOKS WIDE-EYED, MOVING UP-
> STAGE. HIM FOLLOWS]

HER: My dad says the world's a scary place.

HIM: Is that what you believe?

HER: It's what my dad says.

HIM, SHE, HE: Is that what you believe?

HER: The world is – is – big.

> [HIM TIGHTLY CROSSES HIS ARMS ACROSS
> HIS CHEST. SHE APPROACHES.

HIM: My mom says I'll make a great doctor.

SHE: Is that what you want to be?

HIM: It's what my mom says.

SHE, HE, HER: Is that what you want to be?

HIM: I want to write poetry.

> [SHE STAMPS HER FEET. HE APPROACHES.]

SHE: I'm mad.

HE: Mad that?

SHE: I shouldn't do what I think I should do.

HE, HER: Mad that?

SHE: I don't have my mom's approval to do what I want to do.

ALL: Hmmm.

[HE SIGHS DEEPLY. HER APPROACHES.]

HE: I'm sad.

HER: Sad that?

HE: There's no place for me in this world.

HER, HIM: Sad that?

HE: I don't belong anywhere.

HER, HIM, SHE: Sad that?

HE: My dad thinks I'm worthless and no good.

ALL: Hmmm.

[HER RUNS FROM ONE POINT TO ANOTH-ER. HIM FOLLOWS.]

HER: I'm scared.

HIM: Scared that?

HER: If I go into the world it's going to eat me up.

HIM, SHE: Scared that?

HER: I'm dying a little everyday.

HIM, SHE, HE: Scared that?

HER: I'm going to live.

ALL: Hmmm.

[HIM JUMPS ONTO A BLACK BOX. SHE AP-
PROACHES.]

HIM: I'm glad.

SHE: Glad that?

HIM: I could be a doctor if I wanted to.

SHE, HE: Glad that?

HIM: I could be a poet and make readers weep.

SHE, HE, HER: Glad that?

HIM: I can be whatever the fuck I want to be!

**ACTORS PILE ON TOP OF ONE ANOTHER.
TOGETHER THEY PULSATE. AUDIENCE
HEARS THE BEATING OF A HEART. THE
PULSE INCREASES AS THE BREATH OF THE
ACTORS BECOMES PANTING UNTIL THEY
PEAK.**

STAGE NAUGHT
PART ONE: CONNECTING

Age: Prenatal

Before we are born, our main task is to make our first connection to other human beings – our parents – the template we will use for all later attachments in life. It is also important for us to experience ourselves as physical beings with physical needs, feelings and power.

TASKS

In this stage we need to complete some of the following developmental tasks: We need to find a place for ourselves in the uterus, and make our first attachment physically by implanting as embryos in the uterine wall. We must establish a healthy connection to our parents and we need to take in energy, nurturing and nourishment from them. It is our belief that we are sentient and wise beings from the very beginning, and we need to become "conscious" as human beings with body, with feelings, spirit, mind and gender. We need to experience safety, protection, needing, and having needs met in healthy ways. We need to establish a sense of my place, and of belonging. We must experience sensations and feelings, and we need to express them within the limitations of our environment. We must experience being in a physical body through sensations, pleasures, sensuousness, motion and growth.

ABUSE ISSUES

Typical kinds of abuse experienced in this stage include: having a mother who does not want to be pregnant; having a mother who attempts an abortion; growing in a mother who abuses herself physically by use of drugs, poor nutrition, or who is herself abused by others; having a father who abuses his wife, or who is not himself committed emotionally to the pregnancy, etc.

RE-EXPERIENCING THE NEED TO CONNECT AS AN ADULT

Many adults find themselves in emotional predicaments where they have difficulty explaining things to themselves and to their close associates. Some of these predicaments are directly related to the unmet tasks of stages in their early development. For instance, those of us who missed parts of prenatal development will find that we want to be enveloped in a protected and nurturing environment without being directly touched, stimulated or addressed. We may carry sensations of fear and anger in our bodies that we do not recognize as rationally ours. We may experience a desire for bland food, or possess a low interest in eating. Many of the tasks of our adult lives will seem overwhelming. In this respect, we may experience our feelings and sensations as bottomless and totally overwhelming. We may be keenly aware of inner body sensations. We may find ourselves sleeping a great deal and taking many naps or going to bed early and getting up late. The tasks of thinking and solving problems may seem huge and unmanageable. We may experience feeling adrift, alienated, invisible, unconnected to people, not belonging, or not being wholly present. We many have trouble with intimacy, and we may fail to make and keep commitments. Because of an undefined sense that something is missing or a vague feeling of loss, we may see emotional fulfillment through accumulating possessions. We may deny our needs and feelings, have a low awareness of them, or express them inappropriately. We may have allergies or chronic problems in particular body systems, such as diabetes, immune system disorders, or asthma. We may fail to experience the physical pleasures of being and moving in our environments. We may experience gender confusion, suicidal tendencies, and sensations of constant rage and terror.

HEALING RITUALS

The healing rituals, which have been devised for correcting unhealthy prenatal experiences, include a variety of regressive experiences including:

The client is wrapped closely in a sheet made into an envelope by pulling the four corners together while snuggling closely to one or both "new and healthy" parents. The structure of the affirmations given during this time is specific to the prenatal stage that the person is challenging: "This is a healthy place for you to implant and connect." "You move freely and easily." "Your new mother is healthy and takes good care of herself." Any phrases which generate a sense of well being are used at the direction of the client. Should there be archaic feeling states which need to be catharted at this time, the client will become aware of the emotional energy and will do what he needs to do to release it.

"Prenatal rage or fear restraint" is another useful healing ritual focusing for this stage. If there are issues around the umbilical cord or the placenta, these can be focused on and stages in a way that will have deep emotional meaning for the client. Hypnotic inductions and guided imagery are used to deepen the effect of these healing rituals.

The Right to Fly tapes are useful in this as well as other stages.

Two very useful and important rituals for the prenatal and perinatal stages are available in a workshop session. Both **Reichian Breathing** and **Aquagenesis** use a particular physical stimulus to support the client in regressing to the necessary stage, and tapping directly into energy from early traumatic experiences. This results in connecting, catharting expression feelings, and finally, creating new more positive experiences. These sessions generally last from one to two hours for each participant.

Reichian breathing is accomplished through a controlled breathing technique communicated to the client by the therapist through guided imagery and careful coaching. This process is similar to that described by Grof as holotropic therapy. (Grof 1988).

Aquagenesis is conducted in a warm pool or tub where the therapist and others support and protect the client floating, moving as his body dictates and allowing the expression of feelings. Sandy Landsman describes this process in her book Found a Place for Me. (1986).

CASE STUDY

She sensed that while she had incubated in her mother's womb her father had been scared of the bloated belly and pending change in life, so her mother tried to hide it from him. As an adult she was afraid of his fear and discomfort as well as her own. She became confused as to whether or not she belonged in the world. She felt alienated, isolated and alone. Her behavior reflected these feelings. She asked her therapists to be her new dad, and mom, come to her home and hold her in her bed. In his arms she experienced the intense fear of rejection. She was surprised to feel her new dad's loving attention. She expressed her long repressed fear of not being seen, of being invisible, of being unwanted. Her fear intensified until it transformed into joy. In the months that followed this session, she reported that for the first time in her life, she was able to be at home alone consistently without feeling scared or non-existent. She had begun to feel she belonged. She acknowledged her alienation and isolation and was determined to do something about her loneliness.

STAGE NAUGHT
PART TWO: DISCONNECTING

Perinatal

The process of starting labor is a result of the baby releasing the appropriate hormones for the labor process to begin. The baby and the mother work together, in synchrony, to bring about the baby's birth. Anything "going wrong" during this time will result in the baby being imprinted by the particular hardship or other trauma which can occur. It is therefore very important that the baby and the mother be respected in this process and be supported in all ways possible to effect as comfortable a process as is possible for both of them. There are several authors who have written about this, among them Arthur Janov, Stanislas Grof, R.D. Laing, and Thomas Verney. A psychologist, William Emerson, does therapy with newborn babies who have experienced traumatic births.

TASKS

During the birth experience, our major tasks are: to "be ready" for the next stage of becoming. To assist the contractions of the uterus by pushing against the uterine wall, thus helping ourselves in the process of moving down the birth canal. We need to experience the rhythm and pace of the squeezing and relaxing of the uterine muscles. We need to "know" that mother is helping and actively engaged in the process so we get the sense that we are not "doing it all alone". We need to feel that mother is relaxed and competent to process, and that she is well supported in her part of the task. We must be able to move down the birth canal and out in a reasonable length of time so that we do not feel "trapped". It is important that we experience our connection with mother beyond the severing of the cord. We must experience the paradox of disconnecting and yet being connected as safe and easy.

CONNECTING AND DISCONNECTING

[SHE AND HER GO TO THE TOY BOX AND RETRIEVE TWO BALLS. THEY PLACE THEM UNDER THEIR SWEATSHIRTS AND SIT ON THE BOXES. HE LIES IN A FETAL POSITION IN FRONT OF SHE. HIM LIES IN A FETAL POSITION IN FRONT OF HER. HE AND HIM PUT UP THEIR HOODS.]

HIM: BRIGHT AND EXCITED]   Hello – I'm here – wherever that is. Ah, the fluid's fine. Time for a swim. Stroke stroke stroke breath. Stroke stroke stroke. [HER RUBS BALL BELLY.] This is fun. I like it her [FROM A SUPINE POSIITON, KICKS HIS FEET. HER PACES AND RUBS BALL BELLY] Kick kick kick. Yipee! There's that nice rubbing. I like that. [MOVES TO FETAL POSITION. HER SITS DOWN.]

HE: DROWSY AND GRUMPY]   Hello – what the hell's going on? Ah, the fluid's fine. Time for a swim. Stroke, stroke, stroke breath. Stroke, stroke stroke. [SHE FIDGETS.] This is fun. I like it here. [FROM A SUPINE POSITION, KICKS HIS FEET. SHE MIMES GETTING A DRINK OR TAKING A PILL.] Kick kick kick. Yipee! I want to play but I'm so sleepy. [GOES TO SLEEP IN FETAL POSITION. SHE SITS DOWN.]

HER: My baby likes it when I rub my belly.

SHE: I like my baby when it's asleep and quiet. Whatever it takes.

HER: When I get mad about something I let out a great scream or sometimes I'll sing. Then I stroke my baby and let him or her know it's not his or her fault.

35

SHE: I don't get mad. Even if I'm angry, I hold it in.

HER: How do you do that?

SHE: I hold my breath.

HER: Your baby gets what you don't release.

SHE: Says who? You? Who are you, Ms. Mother of the Universe?

HER: [TO THE ETHERS.] Is that in the script?

SHE: It's in my script.

HER: I resent you calling me Ms. Mother of the Universe.

SHE: So what?

HER: I don't like you.

SHE: Big deal.

HER: Excuse me [HER RISES AND SHRIEKS UNTIL SATISFIED. HIM SNAPS AWAKE.] That's better. Baby, let go of something you don't have to hold onto. You're safe. [HIM KICKS HIS FEET.] Good kick. You sure know hot to express your feelings. You are wanted and you are loveable.

SHE: [MOCKING] You are wanted and you are lovable. Do you honestly think your baby understands?

HIM: [TO HE.] I'm going to be healthy and strong.

HE: Spare me, Mr. Baby of the Universe.

HIM: Is that in your script?

HE: Of course, I write my own script.

HIM: That's what you think.

HE: That's what I know.

HIM: I don't like you.

HE: Big deal.

HIM: Excuse me. [FROM A SUPINE POSITION KICKS HIS FEET. HER RISES.] Uh oh. I'm being pushed.

HE: Don't look at me.

HIM: I'm going to be separate soon.

[HER SITS ON FLOOR.]

HE: Not me. I don't want to ever leave here.

HIM: You'll have to sometime.

HE: Not me. I like it here. It's not safe to be out there. I'll stop growing right here thank you. They'll have to cut me out. Or grab me by my feet. Uh oh. [SHE RISES.]

HIM: Got to go!

[HIM DOES A BACKROLL INTO THE ARMS OF HER. SHE MOVES AWAY.]

ABUSE ISSUES

Among the things that can "go wrong" during this stage is being subjected to an induced labor which is not instituted for the baby's or the mother's well being, but for arbitrary reasons such as the doctor's convenience. This kind of intervention will be experienced as a violation because, as we know, babies are sentient beings, they need to be ready for labor to start. Another violation of the baby's integrity at this stage will be the drugging of the mother so that she is not there to work synchronously with the baby in the labor process. Abuse comes in many forms, and if the mother is not prepared for her labor and delivery, if she is frightened and fights it, the baby will experience great difficulty. The process of being removed from the uterus by cesarean section had been recounted in detail: the terror and surprise such a procedure can cause the baby. Since babies are sentient beings, they know the difference between something uncomfortable being done to them for their own or their mother's safety, something done arbitrarily. A classic form of abuse in this stage is the cutting of the cord before it has stopped pulsating. Doing this is terrifying to the newborn infant. Taking the baby away from the parents before it has experienced moments of "quiet alertness" right after birth and has bonded with the parents is extremely abusive. It has resulted in many years of pain and alienation for many individuals. This list of abuses is long and needs to be recognized and prevented.

RE-EXPERIENCING PRENATAL/PERINATAL STAGES . . .

He: [CROSSES TO SPOTLIGHT] Don't look at me. It never really happened. Not all of me was surgically removed. A part of me will always reside in that warm safe place. When I was there I accepted I was unexpected. It didn't seem to matter that I wasn't wanted because I was becoming. Don't look at me. Pass me over, next. Do you know I'm here? Are you looking at me? Do you feel me near? Pass me over, next. I come from far, far away. At least it feels far, far away. Feel? Did I say feel? I didn't know what feel was a minute ago. Maybe I shouldn't know. But I know. Know? Did I say know? I didn't know what knowing was a minute ago. And now I know. Maybe I shouldn't know. Don't look at me. You heard me. Heard? Did I say heard? Don't look at me. You know what I mean. [REMOVES HOOD.] You know how it feels. I am invisible. Don't you see? I walk down the street and get bumped because no one sees me. I'm here but I'm not. I'm present and at the same time, far, far away. My teachers never call on me. They don't look at me, pass me over, next. I am invisible. A figment of the imagination, a piece in a dream, an illusion, a delusion, a shadow, a shade. I never get sick. No one would know how to take care of me. I barely eat. The stomach won't hold anything down, sometimes. I throw up a lot. I spit up, I sneeze, I cough, I fart. I don't take a lot in because it takes a lot to let it back out. I hold onto what I have because there is little of what I am. Sometimes my feelings get lost in the maze between my insides and my exterior. People say I don't share. What's to share? So I serve. I wait tables, providing rare and fancy nourishment for the living. I eat leftovers. My tables hardly know I'm there. They like that. It makes them feel safe and protected. I'm glad. I like to serve.

. . . AS AN ADULT

We may try to stay connected with loved ones beyond what is rational. We may experience panic when at times are suddenly severed. We may push away people who are close to us. We may experience abandonment as life threatening. We may withdraw from loved ones when we most need their presence. We may have difficulty maintaining energy, and experience burning sensations around the naval. We may experience ourselves as unduly vulnerable and need additional protection in our adult activities. Ordinary tasks may seem altogether overwhelming. We may be beset by unknown and unimaginable terrors, and sometimes wish we were dead.

NEGATIVE PRENATAL/PERINATAL MESSAGES

[THE FOLLOWING SPEECHES ARE SAID IN-DIVIDUALLY AND THEN CHANTED TO-GETHER FOUR TIMES AS ACTORS TALK TO DIFFERENT PARTS OF THE AUDIENCE.]

HE: Existence is tenuous, fragile and frail. It's not for everyone.

HIM: Can we get closer? Closer yet? So close we overlap?

SHE: My chest burns, my body burns. I have to move and push and stretch, move and push and stretch.

39

HER: I like the place between sleeping and waking; I can create my own dreams.

HE: [SUDDENLY LIES DOWN] I'm falling! Help me!

[SHE, HER AND HIM GATHER AROUND HE.]

SHE: You can't fall – there's no where to go.

HE: Tell that to the inside of my body. I feel like I'm being sucked down into a vortex at the center of the earth. Intensified sensitivity, feelings larger than my body, I'm drowning. I'm scared, help me, I'm falling. Am I dead?

SHE, HER AND HIM: [TICKLE HE] You're alive, you're alive, you're alive.

HIM: Am I alive?

HE, SHE AND HER: [TICKLE HIM] You live, you live, you live, you live.

HER: Am I really here?

HIM, HE AND SHE: [TICKLE HER] You're here, you're here, you're here.

SHE: Do I really exist?

HER, HIM AND HE: You exist, you exist, you exist.

[HE POSITIONS HIMSELF TO BE TICKLED WHILE OTHERS GRAB ONE OF THE BALLS. PLAY CATCH. HE TRIES TO JOIN THEM. THEY PLAY KEEP-AWAY FROM HE. HE GRABS BALL AWAY.]

40

POSITIVE PRENATAL/PERINATAL MESSAGES

ALL: Script rewrite!

HE: Even if I don't know how, I was put on this planet to connect.

    [HE BOUNCES THE BALL TO ESTABLISH A RHYTHM. ALL MAKE SOUNDS TO ACCOMPANY AND MOVE TO A RAP.]

    I'm here right now
    And I'm here to stay
    I'm here right now
    And I'm here to stay.

    I'm becoming from there
    To here right now
    I'm becoming from there
    To here right now

ALL: Right now?

HE: Right here

ALL: Right here?

HE: Right now.
    I'm becoming a being
    To become right now
    I'm becoming a being
    To become right now

ALL: Right now?

HE: Right here

ALL: Right here?

HE: Right now

ALL: right here right now
right here right now
right here right now
right here right now

HE: I'm here right now
And I 'm here to say
I'm here right now
And I'm here to stay

ALL: Right now?

HE: Right here

ALL: Right here?

HE: Right now

ALL: Hmph

HEALING RITUALS

Some of these rituals cannot be described very easily and are better understood if seen in demonstration. A film by Barbara Findheisen called Journey to be Born shows some of this work. However, the following are two typical rituals.

The participant asks for healthy parents to support a healthy delivery, and sets it up so that the group provides a birth canal with pillows and blankets and their own bodies. The client regresses to the appropriate age and moves through the birth canal to a normal birth. Sometimes before doing a normal birth, the client may need to relive the discomfort of the archaic experience, and will set up all of the circumstances as they are recalled so that the old energy can be released.

Another birth ritual can be carried out in the Aquagenesis or in the Reichian breathing rituals. Often people who are challenging the issues of the pre- and perinatal stages will need to experience two procedures know as "pons stimulation" and "boundaring". These procedures help to access the midbrain and limbic system and assist the client in finding himself sensorily.

CASE STUDY

He carried an overbearing burden of pain and grief. He could not reach the bottom of it in all his digging during the other therapy he had experienced. The grief interfered with his relationships. He had not been able to remain in any one place very long because he found himself perpetually searching for "something that I'm missing". Through the process of listening to himself, listening to his body, and his metaphors, he decided that the issue had to do with being abandoned at birth by a mother who put him up for adoption. He surmised that the delivery had been difficult and that his mother had been terrified by the process of pregnancy and giving birth. He arranged a birth experience in which he releases the old trauma and grief of abandonment. Then he set up another experience with welcoming parents and a gentle birth process. He engaged his whole being in both of the procedures. After this experience he ceased to feel abandoned. He felt bonded to his "new parents" and was able to move on to the other remaining pieces of therapy he still needed to do in order to get his life in the shape in which he wanted it.

STAGE ONE:
BEING

Age: 0-6 months

When we are tiny little babies, our key task is to just BE. In order to accomplish this, we must find ourselves in an environment that supports our BEING. We keep body and soul together, sustain life and learn to enjoy living. We learn to ask for what we want.

TASKS

In her book, Cycles of Power, Pam Levin gives a very detail outline of the tasks, which babies need to accomplish for healthy growth. Basic to these tasks is the existential issue. We need to have our very existence be of supreme importance to key people in our lives. We must be regarded as important aside from what we can accomplish or do. It is essential that we be taken care of in a healthy symbiotic way. Thought for, and supplied for with care. It is imperative that the bond that was established in the previous stage is not broken in any way, that it is continued with depth and sensitivity. We need to touch and be touched, to be treated as sensual and sensate beings. We must be nourished and nurtured for the satisfaction and calming of our nervous systems.

BEING AND NOT BEING

[HIM AND HER SIT ON BOXES READ NEWS-
PAPERS. SHE LIES BEFORE HER. HE LIES

BEFORE HIM. SHE AND HE PUT UP THEIR HOODS.]

SHE: [CRIES LIKE AND INFANT] I'm here, see me. I'm here, see me.

HE: [CRIES LIKE AND INFANT] I want, hear me. I want, hear me.

[HIM PUTS DOWN THE NEWSPAPER TO PICK UP HE]

HIM: What is it, son, what do you want?

HE: This. To be. To be held. To be held and touched.

HIM: I like to hold you, to be near you, to touch you.

SHE: I'm here, see me. I'm here, see me. [HER PUTS DOWN NEWSPAPER, FROWNS, CONTINUES READING] I want, hear me, I want, hear me.

[HER PUTS SHE'S THUMB IN SHE'S MOUTH. IT FALLS OUT AND SHE CRIES LOUDER. HER PUTS BOTH SHE'S THUMBS IN SHE'S MOUTH. THEY FALL OUT AND SHE CRIES LOUDER.]

HER: You always want something and I don't know what the hell it is. I have needs too, you know.

HIM: [TO HE] Your needs are okay with me. You can ask for what you want.

SHE: Hold me, touch me, rock me. [FUSSES LOUDLY]

HER: I don't know what you want!

HIM: Follow your script.

HER: I am.

HIM: Pick her up.

HER: What makes you think you know what she wants? [HER HOLDS SHE WHO STOPS CRYING. HIM MAKES FACES AND SOUND AT SHE AND HE. THEY GIGGLE AND COO] Adults act stupid around babies.

HIM: That's because some of us remember being one. [TO HE] You don't have to hurry; you can take your time.

HER: Easy for you to say. What I would do for a full night's sleep. Sometimes I wish you had never – [SHE CRIES LOUDLY, FOLLOWED BY HE. HIM SOOTHES SHE. HER CLUTCHES SHE TO HER CHEST.] It's all right baby, it's all right. I'm sorry. I love you baby. I'm so so sorry. It's not my fault. I'm so tired, so weary, and one day turns into the next.

HIM: You're doing the best you know.

HER: The sounds, the smell, the boredom.

[HE PUTS SHE DOWN AND WALKS AWAY.]

HIM: To be or not to be, eh?

ABUSE ISSUES

A typical kind of abuse that can be inflicted on the baby at this stage occurs when a baby is ignored. A distinct violation of our integrity is to be treated as if we are unknowing and insentient – like bags of flour – instead of with dignity and respect. Some parents batter hit or shake babies. This is not only damaging to their bodies, but also extremely damaging to their nervous systems. These kinds of behaviors can lock a nervous system into lifelong terror. More subtle abuses that occur at this stage are the ones that arise from parental ignorance. Babies who are breast fed by a contented and calm mother experience safety and trust. Propping the bottle and leaving the baby alone during feeding is abusive.

RE-EXPERIENCING THE BEING STAGE . . . AS AN ADULT

SHE: [MOVES TO SPOTLIGHT.] I want to eat now not when it's time. My tummy hurts – it feels like someone's blowing it up with emptiness. Feed me, Mama, feed me. Papa. What if I'm always hungry, what if I miss my next meal, what if I starve to death? I want to eat but I don't want to have to eat so I won't eat unless I want to which will only be when I can so I won't have to want for that which I cannot have but have what I want because I have it and want what I have because I won't want what I can't have or have what I won't want. I have, I get, I get, I want, I want, I have, I get, I want, want, I want, want. I want your attention because I want your attention and you have to give. I want you to watch me and know I am here because I want. And I want you to want me to want you to watch me. I'm here. Here and now. I'm here and I want. Your attention. I want your attention. Again. I want your attention. Do you like vampires? I love vampires. Since I was a little girl I've loved vampires. I've seen all the movies read all the books. I love them. Sometimes I dream I am a vampire, eternal, immortal with fangs, which hang down my chin. Fangs, long sharp fangs. Vampires never bite their lips. I love them. I do. I love vampires. Only one problem. They suck. They do. Yes, they suck. Unlike me as a baby. I could only eat at certain times and then only from a bottle. No breast. I'm undernourished. It's true. I see it in my work. My best clients are those I talk to over the phone and I know they love me, they do, they say so. They laugh at my jokes and have a good time. But face-to-face I watch them shrink before my very eyes. We go out to lunch and you'd think I was eating them instead of my lunch. They sweat, they twitch, they never say anything, they only sit there with a queasy smile and I know they want to get away so I hasten my pitch but that only alienates them more so

I talk louder, talk fiercer until I'm practically yelling at them and they still look back at me through vacant eyes as though a secret hose under the table was sucking away their sense of being. It's a terrible thing to watch. Vampires. Am I a vampire?

If we reach adulthood with unresolved infant issues, we may experience some of the following: We will have difficulties in our lives around relationships by becoming inordinately mistrustful. We may act as if our sympathetic nervous system is locked in the "ON" position. In other words, we may be in a constant state of fight, flight or freeze. We may be rageful. We will be preoccupied with issues about help about helplessness, trust, mistrust, adequacy, satisfaction and sensuality. We will feel all our sensations with an extreme intensity – exaggerated pain and itching particularly in our mouth, throughout our entire gastrointestinal system and over our skin. We will probably be preoccupied with seeking satisfaction, absent-mindedly drift off, having difficulty concentrating. Sometimes we may be accused of being daydreamers and woolgatherers. We will have intense oral needs chewing our fingernails, pencils, gum or being compulsive about smoking or eating to satisfy a deep gnawing sensation, to quell our emotions. Some of us will rub or scratch ourselves to satisfy our skin hunger and the need for skin stimulation. Along with this some of us may have skin disorders such as eczema, psoriasis and unexplained rashes. We feel as if we have run out of gas emotionally, and need to refuel and reconnect. We want unconditional love and stroking and recognition for who we ARE rather than for our deeds and accomplishments. Even then, words alone may not be effective in satisfying our needs. Some of us like snuggling up close and then we know all is well. Others of us do not trust closeness at all and find ourselves often pushing others away and have difficulty establishing and maintaining long term relationships. We may experience our world as a place of chronic scarcity, feeling that there is never enough time, space, food, money, or love. We may experience a persistent and chronic dissatisfaction and have trouble getting our needs met by others. We may use food to quell feelings and display agitating behaviors such as stuffing food, gambling, and drug and alcohol use. We may consider other self-destructive acts such as outright suicide.

NEGATIVE BEING MESSAGES

[THE FOLLOWING SPEECHES ARE SAID INDIVIDUALLY AND THEN CHANTED TOGETHER FOUR TIMES AS ACTORS SPEAK TO DIFFERENT PARTS OF THE AUDIENCE]

SHE: There's not enough. Why should there be? It's silly to even ask.

HIM: I'm sorry. My fault. I have no right to be here.

HE: It's no good. I'm all alone. Why should I want to get close?

HER: You're in my space. Clear out. Can't tell what's mine from yours.

[SHE SINGS "HAPPY BIRTHDAY TO ME". OTHERS JOIN IN.]

SHE: Do for my birthday? Guess.

HER: You want a surprise party?

[SHE SHAKES HER HEAD.]

HE: You want to go out to dinner?

[SHE SHAKES HER HEAD.]

HIM: You want to go to a play?

SHE: No way.

HER: You want to go to the circus.

[SHE SHAKES HER HEAD.]

HE: You want to go to the zoo?

[SHE SHAKES HER HEAD.]

HIM: You want a one-way ticket to the moon? What?

SHE: Why don't you want to do what I want to do?

ALL: What do you want to do?

SHE: I don't know. I want to get things. I am what I get. My things, my possessions, my treasures are what I am.

HE: I am what I do. My acting, my singing, my dancing are what I am.

HIM: I am what I maintain. My home, my dog, my car are what I am.

HER: I am what I create. My children, my meals, my parties are who I am.

SHE: Is what I get enough to be?

HE: Is what I do enough to be?

HIM: Is what I maintain enough to be?

HER: Is what I create enough to be?

ALL: It is enough to be.

[THEY REPEAT THIS OVER AND OVER, MOVING INTO A CIRCLE. THEY SING RING-AROUND-THE-ROSIES, POCKET FULL OF POSIES, ASHES ASHES, WE ALL FALL DOWN.

THEY FALL DOWN. SHE RISES AND CLAPS
HER HANDS TO ESTABLISH A RHYTHM.]

POSITIVE BEING MESSAGES

ALL: Script Rewrite

SHE: Even if I don't know how, I was put on this planet to be.

       [ALL MAKE SOUNDS TO ACCOMPANY A
       RAP]

       I be here now
       And I'm here to say
       I be here now
       And I'm here to stay
       No umbilical cord
       I be here now
       No umbilical cord
       I be here now

ALL: You are?

SHE: Here now

ALL: Here now?

SHE: I be.

ALL: Hmph

HEALING RITUALS

There are many healing rituals that have been devised for helping persons to challenge their beliefs about themselves and change
them. Among them are any interventions having to do with "being"
issues. Clients working through these issues will structure rituals

having to do with "plenty" and "scarcity" to let them know there is enough – enough love, money, time, etc. – for them.

They will be fed by the therapist, having their feeding paced. They will take a bottle on demand, and they will pay attention to sensations such as touch and skin contact and other nurturant care.

Interactive games are common using such messages as "this is Baby's nose", "this is Daddy's nose", "Mommy loves Baby's skin", being held as a baby and crooned to and so forth.

Reichian breathing and Aquagenesis are also important for "being work".

A client discovering an early decision to "not be" by shutting out feelings and withdrawing may decide to do an "intrusion" ritual. In this procedure, the therapist personifies the healthy parent battling for her child's life. The client acts out the "don't be" and other self-destructive decisions by closing his eyes and pushing the therapist away. The therapist in turn says such things as "this baby won't die", "I want this baby", etc. As this is happening, the group members will be engaged in the Pons Stimulation procedure, lightly rubbing, slapping and deeply massaging the client's arms, legs and trunk.

CASE STUDY

She lived from one crisis to another during an excruciating job search that felt like it was stretching beyond her ability to endure. In therapy she was doing baby work. Regressing to the 0-6 month developmental stage by starting in a prone position, making sounds and movements to indicate she wanted to be held. Previously, she had denied her needs and remained a very quiet, unneeding baby. It had taken months for her to feel comfortable making sounds. It took even longer for her to make sounds that communicated her needs, beginning with a need to be held. It took still longer for her to fuss until she got a bottle or until she was held in the position she wanted to be held. She began to give her voice to her immediate needs.

During the 15 minutes she was held. She moved into a timeless stillness of being. She wasn't asleep, yet she no longer aware of her surroundings. When she was brought out of this state, she felt peace and satisfaction. She no longer longed for the over stimulation and anxiety she felt she needed to feel alive. She became more able to resolve problems before they turned into crises. She reported that she was going into business for herself and had found her marketing plan was already producing desired results.

STAGE TWO: DOING

Age: 6-18 months

The job that we have as a crawler and toddler is to DO. We need to explore our world with our eyes, hands, and our senses by tasting, touching, smelling, seeing, hearing and moving. We can develop our motivation for we're curious, intuitive and ready to find enjoyment in everything we do. We can expand our options for expression and action.

TASKS

In order for us not to get "stuck" in this stage, we need to carry out a number of tasks to prepare us adequately for the next stage of growth. For another way of looking at this same material read Pam Levin's, Sandy Landsman's, and Jean Clarke's books on this same subject.

Our tasks during this period include: to live in an environment that is safe for us to explore without thought for our safety. To live in an environment in which we trust to be the job of parents and caretakers. We need to develop our sensory awareness by doing all kinds of motor and hand-to-eye movements. We need to be able to taste, to touch, to smell, feel and hear what is going on in the world about us. We need to find our balance, first on our hands and knees, then on our own two feet. We need to find our footing, to feel the earth, and to get in touch with the ground –0- to understand what it means to be "grounded". We need to seek a variety of stimulation and to be free to move out into the world. We need to follow our own inner urges instead of what may be socially convenient or responsible. We need to begin to distinguish ourselves from others and to know where we end and others begin. We need to begin to separate from our parents and to experience the power to choose distance and closeness. We need to learn that when people go away, they are not gone forever. We need to learn that our world is a safe place and that we will not be hurt or abused.

DOING & NOT DOING

> [HE TIES A ROPE BETWEEN HE AND SHE AND PUTS UP SHE'S HOOD. HIM TIES A ROPE BETWEEN HIM AND HER AND PUTS HERS HOOD.]

HE: It's okay for you to move out in the world, to explore and experiment.

HIM: You behave yourself.

> [SHE AND HER CRAWL TO AUDIENCE, LOOK-ING IN PURSES, UNTYING SHOES, ENCOUR-AGING AUDIENCE MEMBERS TO PLAY PEEK-A-BOO OR TICKLE. THEY FIND THINGS TO PUT IN THEIR MOUTHS. HE SAYS THINGS LIKE "YOU CAN EXPLORE WHAT'S AROUND YOU", "YOU CAN BE CLOSE OR YOU CAN BE SEPARATE', 'I'M HERE IF YOU NEED ME'. HIM PULLS ON OR YANKS THE ROPE SAYING THINGS LIKE, 'YOU SHOULDN'T BOTHER PEOPLE", "DON'T DO THAT", "GET OVER HERE". SHE GETS SCARED AND CRAWLS BACK CRYING. HER HEARS AND CRIES AS WELL. HIM PULLS HER BACK.]

HIM: What are you crying about? Can't you follow a simple script? That's what happens when you wander off.

HE: Did you get scared? It's okay; I'm here for you. You're safe. It's okay to explore and create your own script.

[SHE STOPS CRYING AND CLIMBS UP HE UNTIL SHE IS STANDING. HER DOES THE SAME. THEY WALK, THEY FALL, THEY HUG THE GROUND AND STAND AGAIN. THEY JUMP UP AND DOWN. THEY LOOK AT ONE ANOTHER. THEY LOOK AT THE ROPES. SHE RUNS INTO THE ARMS OF HE.]

HIM: Don't think about taking off.

ABUSE ISSUES

Among the abusive things that can happen to us when we are in this stage is having to please the grownups and grow up too fast, in order to take care of them. Aside from the obvious kinds of abuse which are inflicted on children this age like screaming at them and hitting them, the most damaging kinds of parenting are too many "NO's". Children at this age need "two yeses for every no". They need a lot of permission to move about and to explore. The "NO word is to be used only in the interest of the child's safety and comfort. Keeping a child in a playpen for long periods of time has been found to be very damaging. Activities, which deny the active use of arms and legs in coordination such as walker chairs and bouncing swings are damaging when used excessively. Being separated from the significant persons in their life without very careful arrangements being made to keep the connection will be damaging. Advice to parents who have to be away for more than a day is to leave a tape with their voice, a picture, and a piece of clothing which smells of the parent, such as an unwashed tee-shirt, or a nightgown.

RE-EXPERIENCING THE DOING STAGE . . .

HER: [MOVES INTO SPOTLIGHT.] I like to suck on five suckers at the same time. Different flavors. I like one, suck on it until I get tired of it, grab another one, put both in my mouth, and pull out the first one. I don't like one better than the other, I like them all, I guess. As long as it's with this special brand of lollipop my dad usually buys. He got me a different kind and I was scared to open them. I didn't know what was inside and I didn't what to know. I knew they weren't my suckers. Oh no. I wonder if my dad was mad at me when he bought them. Maybe he did it on purpose to make me mad. I don't get mad – I'm too scared. I couldn't tell him about the suckers so I threw them away. He bought me more of this same kind. I showed him. I saved them until I had a whole bunch and then I made a sucker flower out of them and gave it to my auntie for her birthday. Boy was he surprised. He's always surprised. [PULLS DOWN HER HOOD.] Me? I hate surprises. They scare me. What if in those moments of unplanned reaction I make a fool of myself? What if everyone sees what's beneath my exterior? They'll know I'm a bad person. What if I display behavior even I don't know about? Who wiould like me then? Last week my dad complained he had to start a new page in his phone book to include my new address. We move around a lot. My kids understand. They know I get restless. They know how fussy I am about my home. We stay in the same neighborhood – that way they continue in the same school. I hate but sometimes it's necessary. I have trouble holding a job for too long - I get bored. Besides, they never pay me enough for all the thinking they want me to do. I'm not scattered – I'm diversified. I'll get it together soon. I just have to do more.

. . . AS AN ADULT:

As adults when we re-experience the doing stage we may run into issues which are related to creativity, motivation, curiosity, intuition, procrastination, eye-hand coordination and locomotion. We may experience conflicts about whether to be passive or to initiate tasks. We use metaphors like the "the ground was knocked out from under me", "I couldn't get my footing". "I feel out of balance" etc. Our attention span is reduced and we have trouble with thinking tasks. We find our urges are more dominant than following through with tasks. Therefore we have difficulty completing tasks we begin. We are sensorialy oriented and want to touch, taste, see, hear, and do something with our world, rather than think about it. We may have difficulty with tasks that require eye-hand coordination. We are told by eye doctors that we have a "lazy eye". We may be afraid of spontaneity, experience blocks in our creativity and procrastinate. We will have low body awareness and poor identification of body sensations. We may have problems with identity, ego boundaries and attachments to others. Depending on the ways we were treated around food and elimination, we may have gastrointestinal and urinary problems as adults. We may experience headaches and eyestrain. Some of us will have allergies, asthma, and skin disorders. Other problems will include muscular coordination and dyslexia. Many of the obsessive-compulsive behaviors are attributed to abuse in this stage of development.

NEGATIVE DOING MESSAGES

[HER PULLS ROPE SO THAT HIM FALLS. THE FOLLOWING SPEECHES ARE SAID INDIVIDUALLY AND THEN CHANTED TOGETHER FOUR TIMES AS ACTORS SPEAK TO DIFFERENT PARTS OF THE AUDIENCE.]

HER: Your feelings make me uncomfortable, keep them to yourself.

HIM: Just hold it, wait a minute, what am I supposed do now?

SHE: I do it all and do it well, perfection – my middle name.

HE: [TO SHE] I couldn't leave if I wanted to. I'm to you forever.

HER: I won a trip to Paris.

HIM: Terrific. Congratulations.

HER: It's not terrific. [HER MOVES AROUND OTHERS. THEY BECOME ENTANGLED.] I'll have to get shots. I'll have to travel for hours on end. I'll have to go where they don't speak my language. I'll have to leave my kids, my home, my life.

[THEY BEGIN TO UNTANGLE THEMSELVES.]

57

HER: Can I learn to separate from others?

ALL: Yes you can.

SHE: Can I learn how to be spontaneous?

ALL: Yes you can.

HE: Can I find secure footing on this Earth?

ALL: Yes you can.

[THEY ARE FREE AND UNTANGLED. HE AND SHE USE ONE ROPE AS A JUMP ROPE. THEY CHANT: LIZZIE BORDEN GOT AN AX, GAVE HER MOTHER FORTY WHACKS, WHEN SHE SAW WHAT SHE HAD DONE, SHE GAVE HER FATHER FORTY-ONE.]

POSITIVE DOING MESSAGES

ALL: Script Rewrite.

HER: Even if I don't know how, I was put on this planet to do.

[HER SNAGS ROPE BUT CONTINUES BEAT TO ESTABLISH A RHYTHM. ALL MAKE SOUNDS AND MOVE TO ACCOMPANY A RAP.]

I do what I do
And I'm here to say
I do what I do
and I'm here to stay

I touch and I grab
I do what I do

I touch and I grab
I do what I do

ALL: You do?

HER: Say what?

ALL: You what?

HER: I do
I'm taking a walk
And I do a little talk
I'm taking a walk
And I do a little walk

ALL: You do?

HER: Say what?

ALL: You what?

HER: I do

ALL: Do wop do wop do wop
Do wop do do
Do wop do wop do wop
Do wop do do

HER: I do what I do
And I'm here to say
I do what I do
and I'm here to stay

ALL: You do?

HER: Say what?

ALL: You what?

HER: I do

ALL: Do wop do wop do wop
       Do wop do do
       Do wop do wop do wop
       Do wop do do
       Humph

HEALING RITUALS

The healing rituals devised for this stage can provide satisfaction and be very rewarding. They include exercises for sensory awareness and sensuousness.

It may be necessary to see a kinesthesiologist for muscle testing and reordering of neuronal pathways that are key to this stage of development.

Another ritual involves taking risks with appropriate protection, such as "being little" and crawling around to explore the environment as a "little one".

Learning to identify the specific feelings of mad, sad, scared, and glad and connecting them to the appropriate body sensations is an important ritual for this stage.

Being messy while playing with food and other appropriate messy things like play dough, finger paints, etc., are helpful rituals.

A common procedure for working on separation issues and boundaries is one in which the "child" clings to the new parent, experiencing the power to keep the parent close. Being tied to the parent with a nice long cord, which gives the feeling of being connected yet separate, has proved to be a very satisfying procedure to date. The traditional game of "peek-a-boo" shows the child that mom or dad is still there, even when out of sight.

CASE STUDY

A young woman became overanxious whenever she was to travel. She liked the idea of exploring unknown territory and getting to know cultures other than her own, but was afraid to carry out the idea. She claimed that she had addressed this idea in other therapeutic modalities and that "nothing had worked". In the face of her fears, she experienced a nagging tension and overwhelming fatigue whenever she had traveled, making it "no fun at all". In most circumstances in her life she was assertive, but while traveling, she was afraid to ask questions, determined to somehow figure out the answers by herself because she was afraid others would notice she didn't belong there. In her therapy she worked at the 6 to 18 month level, crawling and toddling around the room, exploring it, going up to the other group members, asking them questions, asking to be held, asking them to play with her. At first she was hesitant to reach out because she was afraid her needs would be rejected. With practice, she learned that other group members welcomed and even enjoyed their encounters with her so that she felt less and less anxious about initiating interactions with them. Doing this as a "child" made it possible for her to suspend the critical part of her personality and feel free to be spontaneous. Later, she reported her excitement about an approaching trip she was planning, and she was not experiencing her familiar anxiety about it. She could hardly wait to get started. When she returned she reported that her energy level remained appropriate, and she was able to pace her trip and avoid all of the old anxieties. She had remained flexible about asking for directions, and ended up experiencing the trip as joyful and adventurous.

STAGE THREE:
THINKING

Age: 18 months to 3 years

In stage three, we are ready to become independent individuals in our own right. We want to begin using information we've gained from our Doing stage, to find reasons for events, to make sense out of the world around us. We particularly want to feel our own power and to be able to wield it. We have discovered that the word "NO" is a very powerful word, and we want to be able to use it ourselves. We expect that the grownups will respect our "no's" as we are learning to respect theirs. We want to be able to manage our own clothing, make big decisions about what to wear, eat and what to do.

TASKS

We need to challenge our former dependency and need to cling, and see ourselves as separate and whole. We want to play beside someone, not with someone. We must test our limits and those set by others by pushing those limits. This creates space for us to think about boundaries and limits. There are a number of specific tasks for this stage that can be read about in detail in Pam Levin's and Jean Clarke's books. It is important for us to find out our relationship to others. We need to develop concepts, take in information and learn to THINK. We need to find out the limits of ourselves and the world we live in. We need to express negativity and our opposition to others. We need to develop control of our large muscles. We need to establish our independence and exert our own opinions. We need to be able to push against others and find out where their limits are. We must learn more about feelings, not just the worlds and body sensations they generate, by how to use them to break out of our dependency. We need to learn how to think and feel at the same time. Common metaphors are "be independent", "do it all myself," "I'm stuck".

THINKING AND NOT THINKING

> [HE AND SHE TALK QUIETLY. HIM AND HER PUT UP THEIR HOODS. HER PLAYS WITH A TEDDY BEAR. HIM PLAYS AWAY USING FIRST THE AUDIENCE AND THEN HER AS ENEMY.]

HIM: Prisoners.

> [HIM GRABS TEDDY BEAR. HIM AND HER PULL AT THE BEAR.]

HIM: Mine.

HER: No, my bear.

HIM: Mine. Gimme.

HER: No. I want to play with it.

HE: [SARCASTIC] Why don't we play Solomon. I'll get a knife and we can cut it in half so you can both play with it. Would you prefer that?

HIM: I want it back. My dad gave it to me.

HER: But I was playing with it.

HIM: I want it now.

SHE: Bring it here.

HIM: [GRABS ANIMAL] No.

[HER HAS A TANTRUM, FALLS TO THE FLOOR, STAMPING FEET AND HANDS AND SHOUTING "I WANT THE BEAR"]

HER: [TO HER] Quit acting like a spoiled brat.

SHE: [TO HER AND HE] It's all right to let us know you're angry.

HE: You like this racket?

HIM: [POINTING TO SHE] Dad, do you love her more than me?

HE: When you behave like this I do.

HER: [HE GOES TO TOUCH HER.] No.

HE: You should go to your mother. Can't you see SHE cares about you? Don't be ungrateful.

HER: No.

HE: Brat –

[HE MOVES AWAY AS SHE APPROACHES HER]

SHE: You can say no to become separate from me. You can test your limits. I'll still love you.

HER: No.

SHE: Do you want to play paddy-cake?

HER: No.

SHE: Do you want to run around the room?

HER: No.

SHE: Do you want to read a book?

HER: No.

HE: Who writes your script?

SHE: We're improvising. What's wrong with a little "no"?

HER: Ya, what's wrong with a little "no"?

HIM: Can I say "no"?

HE: No. [THEY LAUGH]

HIM: [TO BEAR] It's your fault. [HITS BEAR]

SHE: Are you mad at bear? [HIM SHAKES HEAD] Do you still want the teddy bear?

HIM: I – I --- no. [TO HER] You can play with him. You'll take care of him?

HER: Yes. Yes, I will. [MOVES INTO THE ARMS OF SHE] Look, I got bear, I got bear. I'm gonna take care of bear.

ABUSE ISSUES

The abuses, which we may have experienced as children, aside from what people usually think of – being hit, spanked, yanked around etc. – are commonly the following: we were not respected and treated as dignified human beings struggling to learn a new set of demands instituted by our body's growth, and by the expectations of the culture in which we are grow-ing. We were treated as if we were a "dumb animal" with no thoughts and feelings of our own. We were expected to solve tasks that were beyond our developmental and neurological capacity. Our feelings, our "no's", our ability to think were discounted and over-ridden. We were expected to be toilet trained before we were neurologically ready for the task. We were pushed to "grow up" when we still sometimes felt like a baby and needed to be treated as such. Two year olds need to regress from time to time. It is important that they do because they "know a lot about the baby within". We were not allowed to be separate and connected and find out our own limits and boundaries.

RE-EXPERIENCING THE THINKING STAGE . . .

HIM: [MOVES TO SPOTLIGHT] I am constipated. I take it all in and I take in a little more. But nothing comes out. I want to keep everything so I don't let anything out. Except sometimes. I get pissed. My mother says I am a holy terror. I hide things from her – things she wants to use. I hid the broom in the shower, the vacuum cleaner under the sink, the cleaning stuff in her dresser drawers. Boy does she get mad. I remember the belt. I hated that belt. I also loved that belt. It meant I could do bad things, be punished and then do some more. I never made a sound – not one cry. I always loved hidden mysteries and secrets. I read every Nancy Drew – don't laugh – they were good books, well written. Ya, I take it all in. [PULLS DOWN HOOD] I take in so much I get bloated. I get big. I get hard. I can get it up but I can't always let it out. I dream my feet are in cement and the world goes on around me. I take it ALL in [EXERCISES VIGOROUSLY] I work it out, work it out, work it out so I don't have to think about it. I get mad. And I work it out, work it out, work it out some more. I get pissed. And I work it out, work it out, work it out some more. I rant and rave. And I work it out, work it out, work it out some more. Control is my middle name. I'm like a pressure cooker. I only explode once in a while. Out of my way when that happens. I completely lose control. I throw things. I tear apart whatever or whoever is around me. Or so I'm told. My feelings are so intense I don't remember. My wife calls them blind rages. I have little rages in-between – they come and go before I notice they ever arrived. My wife calls those tantrums. Some loyalty. [RAGING] Sometimes I wonder what she does all day while I work my ass off. She's always got a story, some service SHE's doing, a lunch, cleaning house. She says I'm the only dick in her life. Prove it, I say. [QUIETLY] We have control over our own money. I don't get stuck paying her bills and she doesn't have to pay mine. 50-50 all the way. I love my wife. When I used to get in one of my rages she'd try and analyze whatever was eating me. I hate when other people think they have to do my thinking for me. Now, when I fly off the handle she starts to cry. It breaks my heart. It makes me want to cry too. I hold her and take her upstairs. During our lovemaking, I can't tell where I end and she begins. It's bliss.

. . . AS AN ADULT

Every time we return to stage three in our recycling process, we begin a new level of testing activity. We confront separateness, responsibility, and thinking issues. We find ourselves unduly resistant to others. We feel rebellious and contrary, and wonder at others failure to be compliant. We tend to get into power struggles and control issues. We may become preoccupied with finding or establishing our importance to others. We will want to find the limits to things: how far is far enough? Too far? Where do I stop and you begin? Who's in control? We may clearly want what's "mine" distinguished from what's "yours". We may get into situations where we invite others to think for us, and then become furious if they do. We may experience bouts of stubbornness, forgetfulness, procrastination and greed. We may dream of being stuck and our feet are planted in mud as we struggle to be free. We may dream a lot of babies and take the time to look a lot at babies because age two is when we had to "put the baby away and grow up". We may feel angry for no apparent reason, flying into tantrums, throwing things, making messes as we did when we were two. We may then let go of the anger and forget about it with no apparent resolution while everyone around us is still wondering what is going to happen next. We may get irrationally stubborn, or nastily nice. We will have angry outbursts, discount our own and other's feelings, and try to control those around us by either talking their ears off or by being so silent they end up second guessing us.

We may come across to others as negative, rigid and oppositional. We may be very quick with our "no's" or unable to say "no" when it is appropriate. We may have intestinal problems, tight or lax sphincters, low back pains and tight shoulders. We may have little regard for society's rules and break them regularly by getting speeding tickets, or getting frequent reprimands from authority figures.

NEGATIVE THINKING MESSAGES

[THE FOLLOWING SPEECHES ARE SAID IN-
DIVIDUALLY AND THEN CHANTED TO-
GETHER FOUR TIMES TO DIFFERENT PARTS
OF THE AUDIENCE]

HIM: Careful. Don't make me mad 'cause I get bad.

HER: I'll do it myself, thank you very much.

SHE: Don't you know? I'm right all the time.

HE: Get too close, I rebel, let our contact go to hell.

[ALL APPLAUD]

HE: Did you like what you say?

HIM: It was re – re –

HE: redeeming?

HIM: redeeming in qualities other than those I value and obviously e-- e—

SHE: entertained?

HIM: entertained may even if I wasn't one. It was i— i—

HER: interesting:

HIM: interesting and moved from moment to moment. It showed a
potentially ex—ex—

HE, SHE, HER: expressive?

HIM: expressive mode of –

HE: Did you like it or not?

HIM: I'm sorry. No. Can you say no?

HER: No. Can you say no?

SHE: No. Can you say no?

HE: No. Can you say no?

ALL: No. [HIM JOINS ACTORS AT THE END OF A LINE.
HIM LEADS THEM IN FOLLOW-THE-LEADER.
HIM PUTS HIS HANDS UP FOR PADDY-CAKE AND
ESTABLISHES A RHYTHM.]

POSITIVE THINKING MESSAGE

ALL: Script rewrite

HIM: Even if I don't know how. I was put on this planet to think.

[ALL MAKE SOUNDS TO ACCOMPANY AND
MOVE TO A RAP]

I'm thinking I know
and I'm here to say
I'm thinking I know
And I'm her to stay

Know my limits know yours
I'm me you're you
Know my limits know yours
I'm me you're you

ALL: You know?

HIM: I think

ALL: You think

HIM: I know
I can think about my feelings
I can feel about my thoughts
I can think about my feelings
I can feel about my thoughts

ALL: You know?

HIM: I think

ALL: You think

HIM: I know

ALL: To think to know
To know to think
To think to know
To know to think

HIM: I'm think I know
and I'm here to say
I'm think I know
And I'm her to stay

ALL: You know?

HIM: I think

ALL: You think

HIM: I know

ALL: Hmph

HEALING RITUALS

Since one of the most important functions of this stage of development is the ability to think and solve problems, one of the most important rituals for this stage is the one we call "the accountability contract". In this ritual the client agrees to take time out in the accountability in the "think chair" and think through inappropriate behavior. Frequently the client has engaged in "non-thinking behaviors" and has in some way, broken one of the self-care contracts mentioned at the beginning of this book. When this occurs, the client "goes to the accountability" and thinks about: (See Pages 140 and 165)

1.   Which contract was broken;

2.   How it was broken;

3.   What the underlying script issue is involved in the breaking of the contract, i.e. what the mistaken belief system about self is;

4.   What they think they need to do in therapy to change the mistaken belief system.

The last part involves the client in planning a piece of therapeutic "work" or healing ritual that will directly address the script issue.

The client may choose to do a psychodrama or be a two-year-old with appropriate parenting. They may do the "no" procedure where they respond with "no" to every question asked of them.

Anger is a key emotion for this stage so that a number of the healing rituals for this stage directly address the release of the archaic anger. The client may do a two-year-old temper tantrum on a mat on the floor or do a rage restraint with the assistance of the group and the therapist.

Other rituals for this stage provide the client with opportunity to separate thoughts from feelings, to understand what is his and what may be others' feelings. He learns to think and feel at the same time by receiving caring confrontations for inappropriate behaviors and experiencing the logical consequences for these behaviors.

CASE STUDY

A professional man with a wife and young family was overworked. He wanted a change, but felt incapable of making any career decisions. He reacted to difficult situations by becoming obstinate, unmovable, disdainful, cloaked in silence except for occasional growls through clenched teeth. He blamed the world for forcing him to do things he did not want to do. He would not say "no". Nor would he tell his employees, his colleagues, his family, exactly what his limits were because he would not acknowledge them for himself. He elected to spend time in therapy "being two". As a part of the process he accepted the accountability contract, which required him to spend time out thinking about his inappropriate behavior and resolve the problems behind it. He also elected to do anger work including "rage restraints', and temper tantrums. In both his "play time" and his anger work, he practice saying "no" to his heart's content. His work helped him learn how to say "no" and taught him about setting limits for himself. He learned that he could get his needs met. He learned some ways to take care of and protect himself. After completing the two-year-old work, he reported that his thinking was clearer and more precise. He knew better what to negotiate for himself, his limit setting at work have him more time for his family. The way in which he set limits at home were more reasonable and more thoughtful. His wife reported that life at home was easier, now that he did not have the outbursts he had before. He said he was able to make clearer decisions at work, a great relief for him, and for his associates.

STAGE FOUR: IDENTITY

Age: 3 years to 6 years

Who am I? Who is this person called me? What are my likes and dislikes, my talents, my ethics, my heartbreaks, my desires? Is it okay to be a girl? A boy? To answer such questions is to know who we are.

TASKS

To grow up in a healthy way, we need to find out the answer to "Who am I?" We need to discover what it means to be male or female. We need to test the definitions of reality through logical consequences. We need to exert our power and see how it affects our relationships. We need to separate fantasy from reality, and learn that no, there really is no monster in the closet. We develop the ability to organize and change our internal reality so that it better fits the world in which we live. We need to have lots of friends and learn to build peer relationships. We need to be involved with grownups that respect us and treat us with dignity as we negotiate the difficult tasks of this stage.

IDENTITY AND NON-IDENTITY

[AS VOICE SPEAKS, ACTORS MIME BEING
LED TO A CENTRAL PLAYING AREA BY
A PARENT. THEY WEAR COMFORTABLE
BUT MISMATCHED CLOTHING. THEY ALL

73

WEAR HATS. THE TOY BOX IS REPLACED
BY A MILK CRATE. THEY MAY FUSS, JOIN
THE GROUP ENTHUSIASTICALLY, ETC. HER
HOLDS A STUFFED MONKEY]

SHE: [GRABS MONKEY FROM HER] I'll be the mommy [TO
HE], you be the daddy and you're the kids.

HIM: I don't wanna.

HER: [GRABS MONKEY BACK] And monkey is my baby.

HE: Okay. You come to our house for dinner.

SHE: Ya. Set the table, dear.

HE: Okay.

HER: I'll feed the baby. Where's the bottle?

HIM: My mom doesn't use a bottle. She gives my baby brother her
booby.

HER: Her what?

HE: You know.

SHE: My mom's got two boobies.

HIM: So does my dad – they're real small. But he's got a bigger
weenie.

HER: A what?

HE: You know.

SHE: I don't have one of those.

HE: I do.

HER: I don't know if I do.

HE: You don't know?

SHE: She doesn't. [TO HER] You don't.

HER: I don't. But my Dad likes to show me his. Sometimes he likes me to touch it.

HE: Why? [HER SHRUGS]

HIM: Guess what I got.

ALL: A poster of Magno Maxi Moron. It's in my room upstairs.

HE: Wow! Can I come see? He's my favorite.

HIM: Me too. I want to be just like him when I grow up.

HER: Not me. I want to be a famous actress. Maybe I'll make a movie with Magno Maxi Moron.

SHE: You can't do that. He's a cartoon and you're a real person.

HER: Oh. Can I come see Magno Maxi Moron?

HE: No. He's our favorite.

HER: [TO HIM] I'll let you play with monkey.

       [HER STANDS IN BETWEEN SHE AND HIM]

SHE: You said I could.

HER: You both can.

HIM: Can I hold him now?

SHE: I want to hold him now.

HIM: I'll show you Magno Maxi Moron.

HE: I wanna see Magno Maxi Moron.

SHE: I'm your best friend.

HIM: If you don't let me play with monkey, I won't let you see Magno Maxi Moron.

SHE: If you don't let me play with monkey, I won't be your best friend any more.

HE: [TO SHE] I'll be your best friend.

HER: She's my best friend.

HE: Not anymore.

HIM: [TO HE] You still wanna see Magno Maxi Moron?

HE: Ya. [SHE NUDGES HE] Can she come with? Maybe I shouldn't. My mom might need me. She needs me a lot.

HIM: She's busy with the other parents. Why would she need you?

HE: Because sometimes she does. And if I don't take care of her she gets mean. [HE ABSENTLY RUBS HIS BOTTOM]

HER: [SITS WITH HE] My mom doesn't get mean. She doesn't get anything.

SHE: [GOES TO HIM] Can I come see Magno Maxi Moron?

HIM: Sure.

HER: Me too?

HIM: If you let me play with monkey.

HER: You can play with monkey [HER GIVES MONKEY TO HIM. TO SHE] Will you still be my best friend?

SHE: I don't know.

HE: I'll be your best friend.

HER: [TO SHE] Don't you like me anymore?

SHE: You're so dumb. What's to like?

HER: I don't know.

HE: I like you.

HIM: [MAKES THE MONKEY SPEAK] "Cause you're so dumb."

HER: Gimme my monkey back. [GRABS MONKEY AND HOLDS OUT TO SHE] Here. You can hold him.

SHE: I don't want your monkey. I wanna see Magno Maxi Moron.

HE: Can I hold your monkey?

HER: Why?

HE: 'Cause I like you.

HER: Why?

HE: I must like you. I want to take care of you.

HIM: [TO SHE] Come on. I'll show you Magno Maxi Moron.

SHE: Okay.

HIM: [TO HE] Are you coming?

HER: [TO HE] You wanna hold my monkey?

HE: [TAKES MONKEY] Ya.

SHE: Let's go. [SHE AND HIM MOVE TO MILK CRATE TO PLAY CARDS]

HER: Do you really like me?

HE: Sure.

ABUSE ISSUES

Some of the most frequent abuses of children at this stage are continuations of previous abuses such as physical violence, being shouted at, etc. One of the most frequent abuses at this stage is incest, children as sexual objects for unthinking adults. Another subtle and frequent type of abuse is the expectation of the adults that the child is there to fulfill their needs. This particular abuse often starts before birth, and continues to the point that children of this age expect to "take care of" mommy or daddy, having been thoroughly brain-washed by the time they are six years old. In this stage children will make up a "fantasy nurturing parent" who will rescue them from the abuses of their biological family. If this stage is particularly difficult for a child, he will make decisions based on experience, which do not have a basis in adult fact. These decisions then govern his life in the form of the "script" or core beliefs he writes for himself and plays out unconsciously the rest of his life.

RE-EXPERIENCING THE IDENTITY STAGE . . .

HER: What do you like about me?

HE: [THINKING] I like your monkey.

HER: Am I like my monkey?

HE: Ya. And I'm like Magno Maxi Moron.

HER: What if I were the greatest actress in the world. What if I were so great I could act with cartoons.

HE: What if I were a cartoon and you were my actress.

HER: [ANGRY] You can't be a cartoon. [HER REMOVES HAT. ANGRIER] Why do you always think you can be what you're not?

HE: [REMOVES HAT. DEFENSIVE] You're the one with a thousand personas and no ego.

HER: [STRUCK] Am I so bad?

HE: [POUT] I don't know who you are.

HER: [SEETHING] I didn't think so. [CONCERNED] I don't know who I am either. [TAUNTING] I know who you are.

HE: [ALARMED] You do? [DRAMATIC] I had a dream.

HER: [INQUIRING] Another nightmare?

HE: [SUFFERING] Worse. I almost died.

HER: [SARCASTIC] Too bad you didn't.

HE: [HURT] Thanks a lot.

HER: [SINCERE] It is good to die in dreams. It be like being reborn. It be like shedding your skin.

79

HE: [SNOBBISH] I like my skin the way it is.

HER: [PATRONIZING] So do I. [ALMOST CURIOUS] Do you --?

HE: [IMPATIENT] What?

HER: [SCARED] Never mind.

HE: [ANNOYED] Ask me. Do I what?

HER: Do you find me attractive? [DEFEATED] No, I don't want to know. Forget I asked.

HE: [SNEAKY] I overheard someone say they thought they saw you on a television show.

HER: [EXCITED] Me? Really?

HE: [TWISTING] They thought you were a famous actress.

HER: [THRILLED] Imagine. They thought it was me.

HE: [AMUSED] I just made it up.

HER: [SHOCKED] What?

HE: [AMUSED] I just wanted to see how you would react.

HER: [HYSTERICAL] You don't care about me. You've never cared about me. You don't even see me. I'm just some shadow for the fair-haired boy. You don't have the faintest idea who I am. You're

HE: [INNOCENT] Hold it! I was only kidding with you. Keep the abuse to yourself, please. You know how sensitive I am.

HER: [TAUNTING] If you're so sensitive, why are you impotent? Answer me that, Mr. Man.

HE: [FRUSTRATED] Maybe I don't like girls, have you ever thought of that?

HER: [ALARMED] Are you telling me you're homosexual?

HE: [SUFFERING] No. I don't know. How could I know – I've never tried it. Have you?

HER: [EMOTIONLESS] Yes – but I don't know. I guess I've never really enjoyed sex so it doesn't matter what package it comes in.

HE: [SHOCKED] Then all those fireworks were lies?

HER: [SEDUCTIVE] More like performances to encourage a new reality. Don't be mad at me.

HE: [NEEDY. PUTS HIS ARMS AROUND HER] I'm not. I remember when we first met. I thought, there she is – my voodoo princess – come to purge the darkness that terrorizes my soul.

HER: I remember. I remember I looked at you and thought, my prince charming has come to carry me off to Paradise on his great white horse. [DISAPPOINTED] Some prince charming.

HE: [DISAPPOINTED] Some voodoo princess. [SCARED] Promise you'll never make a doll of me.

HER: You're already a doll. [LAUGHS]

HE: What?

HER: A hippie Ken doll with glasses. [AMUSED LAUGHTER TURNS TO A CACKLE]

HE: Don't laugh at me. I mean it. Why do you always make fun of me?

. . . AS AN ADULT

If we have experienced abuses in this stage, and have unfinished developmental tasks we may continue as grownups having nightmares and being superstitious about our environment. We may count on fantasies such as Prince Charming, or Fairy Godmother to solve our problems. We then have a Cinderella Complex – waiting for the "right" man to show up. We may have sexual dysfunction, such as being anorgasmic, impotent, uninterested in sex, or unresolved about our sexual preferences. We may be compulsive about sex and have many shallow partnerships, never finding satisfaction in our sexuality or in another's. We may be frozen in relation to the functions of our bodies. We may act fragile, scary, or defensive. People around us may find it difficult to have straight, clear transactions with us.

NEGATIVE IDENTITY MESSAGES

> [THE FOLLOWING SPEECHES ARE SAID IN-DIVIDUALLY AND THEN CHANTED TO-GETHER FOUR TIMES TO DIFFERENT PARTS OF THE AUDIENCE]

HER: [LAUGHTER TURNS TO SELF ABUSE] If I think bad things, they have to come true.

HE: When I show I have needs, I'm a sap and a wimp.

SHE: To know I exist I act scary and crazy.

HIM: I don't know who I am, so maybe I'm not.

HER: [ALONGSIDE SHE TO HE AND HER] He said that you said that she said we're turkey heads.

HE: Ya.

HIM: [ALONGSIDE SHE TO HE AND HER] Well she said that you said that he said we're slime molds.

SHE: It's true.

HE: And they said that you said that we said you're slug butts.

HER: You tell 'em.

SHE: And they said that you said that we said you're scum puppies.

HIM: That's right.

HER: Am not.

HIM: Am too.

SHE: Am not.

HE: Am too.

HIM: Am not.

HER: Am too.

HE: Am not.

SHE: Am too.

HIM: [TO HE INDICATING PENIS] I'm bigger than you.

HE: Am not.

HIM: Am too. Am too.

HE: So what?

SHE: [TO HER INDICATING BREASTS] I'm bigger than you.

HER: Am not.

SHE: Am too. Am too.

HER: Who cares?

HE: [TO SHE] I'm smarter than you.

SHE: Am not.

HE: Am too. Am too.

SHE: Big deal.

HER: [TO HIM] I'm better than you.

HIM: Am not.

HER: Am too. Am too.

[THEY PADDY-CAKE TO THE FOLLOWING]

HIM: Someone stole the cookies from the cookie jar –

SHE: He stole the cookies from the cookie jar.

HE: Who me?

SHE: Ya you.

HE: Couldn't be.

ALL: Then who?

HE: Her stole the cookies from the cookie jar.

HER: Who me?

HE: Ya you.

HER: Couldn't be.

ALL: Then who?

HER: Him stole the cookies from the cookie jar.

HIM: Who me?

HER: Ya you.

HIM: Couldn't be.

ALL: Then who?

HIM: [POINTING TO SHE] She stole the cookies from the cookie jar.

SHE: Who me?

HIM: Ya you.

SHE: Couldn't be.

ALL: Then who?

[THEY CONTINUE TO CHANT "THEN WHO"]

POSITIVE IDENTITY MESSAGES

ALL: Script rewrite.

HE/HER: Even if we don't know what it is, we've got power and identity.

[ALL MAKE SOUNDS AND MOVEMENTS TO ACCOMPANY A RAP]

We're a power, we're a force
And we're here to say
We're individuated
And we're here to stay

HER: I'm a girl.

HE: I'm a boy.

HE/HER: We have identity.

HER: I'm a woman.

HE: I'm a man.

HER/HE: We have identity.

HIM/SHE: You do?

HE/HER: We do

HIM/SHE: Move Out?

HE/HER: Move through
We got fantasy, reality
We differentiate
We can make connections happen
We can blow them into space

HIM/SHE: You do?

HE/HER: We do.

HIM/SHE: Move out?

HE/HER: Move through.

ALL: Be in be out
       Be over under through
       Be in be out
       Be over under through

HIM/SHE: We're a power, we're a force
           And we're here to say
           We're individuated
           And we're here to stay.

HE/HER: You do?

HIM/SHE: We do.

HE/HER: Move out?

ALL: Move through.
       Hmph

HEALING RITUALS

Among the healing rituals, which are useful for grownups renegotiant-ing the identity stage, are script re-decision work, and parent interviews. In this work, the therapist helps the client come to clarity about early decisions he may have made. A ritual, which has been found to be useful, is to bring family pictures and talk about the family members as if the client were four or five years old. Psychodrama is a very useful procedure as the client can set up old family scenes and replay them as they aware and as they might have been better. Regression rituals with toys, books and dolls and stuffed animals can be helpful. Learning about sex and sexuality and where babies come from is often done very effectively with the children's books <u>Show Me</u> and <u>Where do Babies Come From?</u>, and <u>The Birth Book</u>. This is a

87

good stage for learning the difference between sexual touching and nurturing touching.

CASE STUDY

A woman in her thirties was having difficulty with sex; she was unable to reach orgasm either with her husband, or with a lover with whom she had been experimenting. In therapy she regressed to four years of age. She searched through the toy box for a set of dolls to represent a family of four. She had the little girl doll ask the therapist questions about her sexuality, sensuality, and sexual identity. At one point the client burst into tears and climbed into the therapist's lap. She sought reassurance that asking such questions and knowing the facts about sex did not mean that she was a "bad" girl. In another session she regressed to three and looked at the book Show Me with the therapist and other little ones, asking questions typical of a three year old. Through this work she recalled an incest experience with an uncle when she was three. After the two sessions she reported that many of her fears about sex had cleared up and that she had experienced orgasm with masturbation. She went on to deal with the incest and after clearing that up, she was experiencing good sex with her husband and had dropped the lover.

STAGE FIVE:
SKILLS DEVELOPMENT

Age: 6 years to 12 years

In this stage, we learn by doing useful things, and by finding how we can be as useful to our family and community. We plant gardens, learn to see, make bread, chop wood, sell lemonade, and deliver newspapers amount the many skills to be learned in our various cultures. We want to know how other people do things, but we may argue about the way they do it, trying to find our own way. We pick people to imitate so that we can incorporate the necessary skills to reinforce our personal power.

TASKS

Developmental tasks for this stage include: The need to experiment with different ways of doing things; the need for the freedom to do things our own way, to learn from our own mistakes; the need to develop physical, intellectual, emotional and social skills; the need to argue, hassle and disagree in order to better understand our and others' limits. The need to exclude our parent's ways of doing things so that we can make our own; the need to develop morals, manners and values we can live by.

SKILL AND NO SKILL

[ACTORS WEAR THEIR HATS. HER AND SHE OIL THEIR ROLLER SKATES, REVIEW THEIR CONDITION, PUT THEM ON AND

LACE THEM UP. HE AND HIM SQUEEZE LEMONS INTO A PITCHER OF WATER. HER IS CAREFUL AND DELIBERATE IN HER AC-TIONS. SHE SHOWS LITTLE PATIENCE FOR THE PROCESS, WATCHING AND FOLLOW-ING HER. HE IS NEAT AND PURPOSEFUL, PLACING THE LEMON RINDS IN THE PROP-ER CONTAINER WIPING HIS HANDS ON A TOWEL, ETC. HIM SLOPPILY SQUEEZES THE LEMONS, THROWS THE RINDS INTO THE SAME CONTAINER BUT MISSES HALF THE TIME. WIPES HIS HAND ON HIS PANTS, ETC.]

SHE: Are you sure I can do this?

HER: No – but you might as well try.

SHE: Will you show me everything you know about skating?

HER: It won't make a difference – you gotta learn yourself.

SHE: But I'll make mistakes, I'll fall down. I'll look stupid.

HER: Like I said, you gotta learn yourself even if you look like the biggest idiot in the universe.

HIM: Who's idea was this anyway?

HE: Yours.

HIM: That's just it – I'm the idea man – I make the plan. My hands sting. Can we be done now?

HE: Why don't you get the cups set up in the box. I'd rather make the lemonade my way anyways. When dad makes it, he uses too many lemons – my mother doesn't use enough sugar. I'll do it just right.

HIM: And I'll sell 'em – you'll see. Should we charge 10 cents or 15?

HE: A quarter.

HIM: I don't know.

HE: It's worth a quarter. I figured it out – wanna hear?

HIM: That's okay, I believe you.

SHE: Help me stand up. Are you sure I can do this?

HER: I want to do a show for our families and all the kids in the neighborhood. It'll be cool.

SHE: But --- but – [THEY DO AN IMPRESSIVE MOVEMENT] Cool. Ya, cool.

HE: [POURING LEMONADE] I'm only pouring a few – just for starters.

HIM: But I'll sell them all.

HE: Then come back for more. I'll be ready for you

[HER AND SHE STRUGGLE TO DO A SHORT ROUTINE. AT SOME POINT, SHE NOTICES A "NEIGHBOR" WALKING PAST]

SHE: Mrs. Cleaver, Mrs. Cleaver, come see what we're doing. Tell us what you think? Mrs. Cleaver, please.

[SHE GOES INTO AUDIENCE AND RE-TRIEVES A "MRS. CLEAVER" TO WATCH SHE

AND HER PRACTICE. HER IS RESPECTFUL BUT VERY BUSY WITH THE CHOREOGRAPHY. AT THE SAME TIME, HE CLEANS UP AND PREPARES MORE LEMONADE. HIM TAKES ON CHARACTERS FROM MOVIES AND TELEVISION AS HE MOVES THROUGH THE AUDIENCE SELLING LEMONADE IF REFUSED. HIM ELICITS FEEDBACK IN REGARDS TO HIS PERFORMANCE. HIM ASKS THOSE WHO BUY A CUP ABOUT HOW IT TASTES. HIM AND SHE COME TO A NEAR COLLISION AND HIM RETURNS TO HE FOR MORE LEMONADE. SHE SEES ANOTHER NEIGHBOR PASSING BY]

SHE: Mr. Rogers, Mr. Rogers, come see, come see.

[SHE RETRIEVES A "MR. ROGERS" FROM THE AUDIENCE AND PROCEEDS GAINING HIS APPROVAL AS HER CONTINUES TO CREATE. HIM CONTINUES TO SELL LEMONADE TO THE AUDIENCE FOLLOWING ANY BIT OF ADVICE AN AUDIENCE MEMBER MIGHT SUGGEST IN HIS NEED FOR FEEDBACK. HE TALKS TO AUDIENCE MEMBERS CLOSE TO HIM ABOUT HOW TO MAKE THE BEST LEMONADE. SHE ASKS "MRS. CLEAVER" AND "MR. ROGERS" RETURN TO THEIR SEATS. AGAIN SHE AND HIM COME CLOSE TO A COLLISION. HE FILLS MORE CUPS. AS HIM MOVES TOWARDS AUDIENCE, SHE BARRELS INTO HIM.]

HIM: You idiot – who taught you to skate?

SHE: What's all this sticky stuff? Ow, I skinned my knee and it stings real bad. Why'd you have to be here? [LICKS HAND]

Hey – this tastes good – but it needs more sugar. [HE GETS ANGRY]

HER: Can I have some? I'm thirsty.

HE: More sugar? I'll show you more sugar.

[HE THROWS SUGAR ONTO SHE AND HIM]

HIM: Cut it out! Look at this mess. I'm the idea man – I don't clean messes. Besides, whenever my mom drinks too much I'm the one who had to clean her up. Sometimes she barfs all over the place. It's gross.

SHE: I know what you mean. I can't go out before I do my chores. Last Saturday, I had to clean the oven, wash the windows, and rake leaves. I was so tired I didn't even want to play. Then I had to baby-sit my stupid sister. She doesn't know anything.

HER: You guys are disgusting. Your dandruff is all over the place.

HE: Ya. Maybe they need a lemon shampoo.

HER: Ya.

[HE AND HER POUR LEMONADE OVER THE HEADS OF HIM AND SHE WHO PULL THEM DOWN INTO THE MESS]

HIM: We'll see who gets a lemon shampoo.

[THEY HASSLE, PLAY, MAKING A LARGER MESS UNTIL THEY ARE ALL ROLLING ON THE FLOOR LAUGHING]

SHE: Sh ... Sh ... Sh ... [THEY QUIET DOWN] Will we get in trouble?

HE: I didn't make the mess.

SHE: You never make a mess. Teacher's pet, teacher's pet.

HE: I can't help it if I'm better at school than you.

HIM: You could pretend.

HER: No he can't. It's not his fault he's so smart.

HIM: I hate school. I never learn anything. I want to [ALL MOAN]
       – honest, I want to learn. But I can't learn the way they want me
       to learn.

HER: I don't care. I'm going to be a prima ballerina so it don't
       matter.

SHE: I gotta do the fourth grade again. I guess I was bad.

HE: I don't think you're bad.

SHE: My mom does. She never talks to me and when she does, she acts
       like I'm a baby who doesn't know anything about anything.

HIM: Except cleaning up.

SHE: Ya – I'm the stupid maid.

HER: My mom says I can learn to do anything I want if I set my mind
       to it.

SHE: My mom says she'll probably be able to talk to me when I'm older
       and understand better. When will that be? I already understand
       a whole bunch of junk.

HE: I'm gonna take this stuff home. How much did we make?

HIM: Hey, I'm the number's man. I'll split it. [HE SPLITS MONEY BETWEEN THEM]

HER: Maybe we should sell tickets to our performance.

SHE: Ya. I can do that.

HE: That was fun until she [POINTING TO SHE] ruined everything.

SHE: It's all my fault, I know.

HIM: We each made – let's see $ _____

HE: O brother. [MOVES TO MILK CRATE]

HIM: I'm afraid if I make a major move it'll get messier.

HER: I have to go wash up. I'm all icky.

SHE: What about our show?

HER: Well – some of it we'll do together and sometimes I'll do a solo. How's that?

SHE: Can I do a solo too?

HER: Sure. [MOVES TO MILK CRATE. HER AND HE PLAY CARDS]

HIM & SHE: Bye.

ABUSE ISSUES

Alice Miller is one of the most important authors to detail how children are abused in our society. (Her three books are listed in the bibliography.) A common form of abuse at this stage occurs when grownups discount the fact that a child this age is thoughtful, struggling to figure out his place in the structure. At the same time grownups tend to neglect children at this stage because they appear quite competent in managing their daily routines and because they often act like "little adults". The subtlest form of abuse, the one least recognized occurs, when grownups believe and expect these children to serve them. When the grownup acts out the needs of his or her own regressions it is damaging to their children. A frequent form of abuse involves the child being expected to carry out the household routines as if they were the live-in maid. Expectations that children this stage will raise the younger children is another form of abuse to both the older child and to the younger one. More obvious abuses include incest, beatings and other inappropriate behavior on the part of adults. Many of our clients have been sexually abuse by their music teachers or by a close friend of the family; frequently it is people in whom the parents have trust to treat their children with regard. Unfortunately, school can often be abusive in that many curricula are not structured to meet the children's learning needs, or teachers who don't like their jobs take it out on the children. Many learning disabilities and conditions of low self-esteem have arisen from abusive school experiences.

RE-EXPERIENCING THE SKILL DEVELOPMENT STAGE . . .

HIM: Now I'm really scared to move.

SHE: What's the big deal?

HIM: If my dad saw this . . .

SHE: My mom wouldn't care. She probably wouldn't even notice the mess if I was in the middle of it.

HIM: We're in the middle of it, all right.

SHE: Just pretend I'm your mom and your dad's coming home in 10 minutes. It'll get clean in no time.

HIM: I know my mom and you're not my mom. In fact, if you were my mom, you'd be grabbing at me trying to hold me as tight as you could or crying with tears and snot running down your face or screaming for another drink. And you know the worst?

SHE: What?

HIM: I do all the cleaning up. Put her to bed and the next morning she don't even remember it happened.

SHE: I don't think my mom even remembers that I happened. At least you got a dad.

HIM: No I don't. I gotta ghost dad. [SHE LAUGHS. HIM GETS FIERCER] He travels a lot. And when he comes home, he drinks with mom. He – he – shows me his belt a lot.

SHE: And I thought you just fell down all the time.

HIM: [PULLS OFF HAT AND GETS UP] What's the best way to handle this? We're two reasonable adults – at least one of us is – I'm sorry I slapped you – it happened before I could stop myself. [GOES TO GET A MOP]

SHE: [PULLS OFF HAT] You're only sorry that when I pulled you down, you brought the lemonade and the sugar with you, you klutz.

HIM: I am not a clumsy oaf – I have more grace in my little finger than you have in your entire body. [CLEANS MESS]

SHE: Do you know that whenever you get angry your eyebrows go like this your mouth – [DOES AN IMITATION OF AN ANGRY HIM]

[SHE DRAWS PICTURES IN THE SUGAR ON THE FLOOR.]

HIM: Would you get the fuck out of there and quit playing with the sugar?

SHE: [SARCASTIC] Yes, dad.

[HIM SWATS HER WITH MOP. HIM CLEANS UP FURIOUSLY]

SHE: Do you think other couples are as happily married as we are?

HIM: What is that supposed to mean?

SHE: Are we normal? Do other people swat their partners ass with a mop for drawing pictures in the sugar that spilled while they were accidentally beating the crap out of each other? Why do people get married anyways? Why do we live in this house? Why do we live on this planet? What are we? Where did we come from?

HIM: Is this some premenstrual existential crisis or are you deliberately trying to drive me insane?

SHE: Why be redundant?

HIM: I wonder what your therapist would think about how you're behaving at this very moment. He'd probably consider it a major set-back.

SHE: You leave him out of this. He knows more about me than anyone – more than you. Besides I trust him. He takes care of me – unlike some people I know. [WATCHES HIM CLEAN] Thanks for cleaning up. [HIM STOPS TO STARE] Do you forgive me? I know I make you mad. Will you forgive me anyway? Will you, will you, will you?

HIM: [CIRCLING AROUND SHE] Maybe we should move to another city. Or maybe we'd do better if we got different jobs.

[HOLDS HER FROM BEHIND] Maybe it's time to start a family.

SHE: [SCARED] Or maybe we should just get a dog.

HIM: [MOVES AWAY EXCITED] That's an idea. Let's get a dog.

SHE: [PICKING AT HIM] I'm scared you'll pay more attention to the dog than to me. You can't. Promise you won't. Promise, promise, promise . . .

HIM: [MOVES AWAY] I hate it when you beg. I'd rather you fight me than beg. It's bad babe, real bad.

. . . AS AN ADULT

When we are recycling the skills stage we may become literal and argumentative, like an eight-year-old lawyer. We may feel clumsy and awkward as if we are growing too fast for our coordination to keep up with the size of our bodies. We may make frequent mistakes as we try out new ways to make things work. We may crave contact with people outside of our usual circle of friends, family, associates, finding out how other people do things. We may become fascinated with the corner of a mouth, the droop of an eye, the move of a hand, the sound of a voice, the manner of speaking, the subtlety of response. We may ask questions like: How do I structure my day, week, year, life? What is important? Are the same things important to you that are important to me? Why do you live here instead of there? Do you like your job? Why have you chosen that way of life? We may be preoccupied with the authorities of our lives – the boss, the minister, the rabbi, the lawyer, the judges, mothers, guides and experts. We may pursue arguments: "I'm sure the rules are not as you say. In fact, I read about that the other day. And besides, my friend told me, and furthermore, when I was little and besides, my mother always . . . "We may search out new social roles, "When I grow up I want to be." "I am tired of staying home with the kids, I think I'll get a job." "This work's too taxing and besides, I miss the kids. I think I'll find an easier line of work." "I know I'm not ready to be a father." "I'm ready to be a student." When we have missed parts of this stage, we may discount our own performance as not good enough. We may be competitive, and uncomfortable about learning new things, become inflexible in our value systems. We may become fearful about our sexuality in relationship with others of the same sex. Metaphors, which are commonly used by us, are: "people say I am argumentative", "I need to know more", "I'm not good enough".

NEGATIVE SKILLS DEVELOPMENT MESSAGES

[THE FOLLOWING ARE SAID INDIVIDUALLY AND THEN CHANTED TOGETHER FOUR TIMES AS ACTORS TALK TO DIFFERENT PARTS OF THE AUDIENCE]

SHE: I'm bad, I'm bad, I know I'm bad. And I'm getting even worse.

HIM: I know you're wrong, those aren't the rules. And furthermore, besides and but –

HE: I'll move, I'll stay, I'll work, I'll play. I've got to start living my life.

HER: I screw it up so I can fix it up. How else will I learn to do it right?

SHE: It's the doom and gloom show!

HE: Big money – big money!

ACTORS TALK ABOUT THE AUDIENCE AS THOUGH, UNLIKE THEMSELVES, THEY LIVE THE IDEAL LIFE WITH PERFECT HAPPINESS. THEY TAKE TURNS TELLING STORIES SO THAT THEY SUFFER AND COMPLAIN ABOUT THEIR OWN LIVES. ACTORS COMPETE FOR SYMPATHY AND PITY]

SHE: [TO AUDIENCE] Let's take a vote. Clap your hands for the person whose life is the worst.

HE: How many of you think my life is the worst?

SHE: And me? How many of you think I have the worst life?

HER: Obviously mine's worse. How many vote for me?

HIM: No comparison. Show them what you know. [INTIMIDATING THE AUDIENCE] Go on, clap your fucking hands.

SHE: Aren't we the worst?

POSITIVE SKILLS DEVELOPMENT MESSAGES

ALL: Script rewrite!

HIM/SHE: Even if we don't know how, we were put on this planet to learn skills and develop talents.

[ACTORS MAKE SOUNDS AND MOVEMENTS TO ACCOMPANY A RAP]

HIM/SHE: We're learning how to do stuff
And we're here to say

HIM: I have my way

SHE: I have my way

HIM/SHE: And we're here to stay.

SHE: I trust my feelings to guide me

IM: I think before I do

SHE: I have ethics

HIM: I have methods

101

HIM/SHE: Always learning something new

HE/HER: You learn?

HIM/SHE: We do

HE/HER: Make it work?

HIM/SHE: Do you?

SHE: Sometimes you're right

HIM: Sometimes I'm wrong

HIM/SHE: So what, big deal, we grow

HIM: Sometimes you're right

SHE: Sometimes I'm wrong

HIM/SHE: So what, big deal, we know

SHE: I don't trust you.

HIM: I learn integrity; I don't see you, let me see you

SHE: Back to reality

HE/HER: You learn?

HIM/SHE: We do

HE/HER: Mistake to learn
Learn to mistake
Mistake to learn
Learn to mistake

HIM/SHE: We're learning how to do stuff
And we're here to say

HIM: I have my way

SHE: I have my way

HIM/SHE: And we're here to stay.

HE/HER: You learn?

HIM/SHE: We do

HE/HER: Make it work?

HIM/SHE: [TO AUDIENCE] Do you?

ALL: Hmph

HEALING RITUALS

Doing a regression in this stage allows the client to set himself tasks that he can finish so he can get strokes for doing good work. Playing table games, arguing and hassling with parent figures, making things and building with Lego Blocks and Tinker Toys are valuable, especially with the parenting figure to act in healthy ways with the behaviors and the contracted acting out. Any experiences, which will give the client permission to disagree, to solve problems without suffering, and to get things done without being hard on them, are useful. Sometimes he will be given homework assignments such as going to the zoo with a friend who assumes the parental role and experiencing being there and having a good time without suffering. So many of us learned to pout and sulk at this stage, that it is important to find out that it is possible to do and be who we are without unhealthy behaviors.

CASE STUDY

A thirty-five-year-old man was experiencing difficulty in making and managing money. He was concerned about bankruptcy in his business because he had mismanaged his money for several years. In therapy he decided to work as a nine-year-old because he felt scared when others in the group worked at that age. Being scared of someone else's work is often a good indication that you have the same issue.) As a nine-year-old he recalled a scene with his parents where he had tried to tell them that he was not happy with his school situation and that he felt his teacher was abusing him. His parents had discounted his efforts and refused to intervene in his favor. The incident had been particularly painful for him and he had resolved he would never again ask his parents for anything. Nor would he tell them anything that was important to him. Soon after the incident, his father was killed in an airline accident. At this point he had decided that being like his father in any was including being successful in business was hazardous and not worth the effort. As an adult he was angry with his mother for inheriting all of his father's insurance money. He expressed his anger repeatedly persuading her to bail him out of fiscal trouble. A recovering alcoholic, he had used alcohol to deaden his psychic pain and feelings. Doing nine-year-old work allowed him to reopen the old scenes. He was more able to clarify his childhood decisions and make some new adult decisions that were more rational and more in his best interest. He began to recognize earlier issues that fed and strengthened his resolve to get even with his mother. He contracted to do the necessary work to resolve these other issues. He closed out his business, got a good job, and began to take personal responsibility for his life and for his money.

STAGE SIX:
REGENERATION

Age: 13 years to 19 years

When we go through the years from age thirteen to nineteen, we will recycle every developmental task and stage of the first thirteen years of our lives. The focus of this stage is regeneration. We will do this in two ways. First, we routinely experience the six previous stages of our lives, from prenatal through thirteen. This recycling gives us the opportunity to pick up any lost threads, redo things that did not get done the first time around. We can renew, restore, and grow new levels of being, doing, thinking, and skill development from our old levels. At the same time, we develop the ability to give birth to others. In this stage we need to accomplish many things in order to develop our own power of regeneration.

TASKS

Among the tasks that face us are the ability to integrate being sexual with needs from other stages. We need to differentiate between nurturing and sexual touching. We must outgrow our parenting relationships. We need to know who we are as sexual beings, and make our sexual identifications. We need to develop a personal philosophy. We revisit and need to refinish each earlier stage. We look to develop our place among the grown-ups.

[HE READS CATCHER IN THE RYE. HIM PLAYS A VIDEO GAME. HER AND SHE GIGGLE. ALL WEAR HATS]

SHE: Is that him?

HER: Don't look so obvious. Yes, isn't he cool?

SHE: Sure he is. And he's made it with half the graduating class. What do you need him for?

HER: I want to meet him, that's all. Jealous? [SHE SHRUGS. HER POINTS TO HE] Maybe He'll introduce me to Him.

SHE: He hardly knows any other humanoid exists.

HER: In algebra, the teacher moves up and down the rows for answers to problems. He's be skipped over at least 10 times. And he's the one who always has the right answer.

SHE: He works at his parent's store. You know, the one near my mom's house? I go in there and half the time I don't even see him until he gives me one of those wimpy "hello's". He gives me the creeps.

HER: It would be bad not to really exist. But I still want to know about Him. [MOVES TO HE. SHE FOLLOWS] Hey, like do you know that hunk?

HE: [ABRUPTLY TAKEN FROM HIS BOOK] What the fucking shit do you want, cunt? [SHAKES HIS HEAD] Ooops. I'm sorry. I didn't mean it – it's the book.

SHE: Come on, let's get out of here.

HER: Oh, stop it, it's cool. Uh – I was wondering – uh – if maybe – do you know – [POINTS TO HIM]

HE: Sure [YELLS TO HIM] Hey, my man. I said, hey, guy. Fucking shit [GOES TO HIM] I'm talking to you.

HIM: Did you say something? What's happening? Wait – I already paid for that gram.

HE: [INDICATING HER] She wants to meet you.

HIM: Check it out. [SEDUCTIVE] Hey pretty little lady.

HER: Hello. Can I watch you play?

HIM: Watch? Ya, sure, baby. Watch me do my thing.

SHE: [TO HE] Cute, aren't they?

HIM: I' a thing doer, know what I mean? I mean, I'm gonna do things j—lots of things. Check it out. [HER WATCHES HIM PLAY]

SHE: I don't get it. I thought she and I were best friends. What does she need him for?

HE: Don't you like boys?

SHE: [ANGRILY] Do you?

HE: I – I [STARTS TO READ]

SHE: Have you ever been out on a date? I haven't. I could care less about going out with some guy. Why am I telling you this?

HE: Because I'm no one.

SHE: Do you really deal?

HE: Why not? I'll never get caught. I'm invisible.

SHE: What if I never have a date? What if I'm always all alone. I'll never get what I want – I'll never get what I need. I'll spend my life chasing phantoms and ghosts. Have you ever had sex?

HE: I – I – [ABRUPTLY READS]

SHE: One minute I'm having bizarre fantasies about men and women, men and men, women and women, touching, kissing, grabbing [HE MAKES A SOUND] and I get real excited. The next minute I think, how gross and disgusting, why would anyone every want to do that? Know what I mean?

HER: You play real good. Do you think you could teach me how to do it?

HIM: [HOLDS HER] Sure, baby, I can teach you how to do it.

HER: [BREAKS FEE] I mean the video game.

HIM: Sure, baby. This is the joystick. You just grab it with both hands, like this, and hold it real tight. I'll help you.

SHE: What's the book?

HE: Nothing. You wouldn't like it. It's for boys.

SHE: What do you mean?

HE: Trust me. Girls hate this book.

SHE: You're total sexist. [MOCKING] You wouldn't like it – it's for boys. I mean, like why are there boys? It's like we're two different species.

HER: You're crazy.

SHE: My shrink says all teenagers are insane. I say all teenage boys are aliens from another planet.

HIM: You're doing real good. I'll be right back. I gotta take a piss. [MOVES OFF]

SHE: [GOES TO HER] Bored yet?

HER: I never knew love could be so wonderful. If he were to ever leave me, I would have to kill myself.

SHE: Hold it. I've never seen you like this.

HER: [AS HIM RETURNS] Hurry – get out of here. He's coming back. I must spend every moment I can with him. I've discovered a totally new way of feeling. It's what adult's must feel. Go on – get – [TO HIM] I'm still here.

HIM: [SHE MOVES TO HE. HIM TAKES HER IN HIS ARMS] I want you baby. [KISSES AND STROKES HER WITH GREAT PASSION] I want you. Do you understand what I say? Let's do it, baby, let's do it.

HER: [PULLS FREE] Not yet.

HIM: [PULLS HER TO HIM] I know you want it, baby. I know you do.

HER: [PULLS FEE] No. I mean yes – but not yet. Give me a little time.

HIM: [PULLS HER TO HIM] But there is not time, baby, only you and me and everything we can do to each other.

HER: [ANGRILY PULLS FREE] I said no. I meant no. Hear me, shithead? I said N-O no! [CRIES AND GOES TO SHE. HIM CROSSES TO HE]

HE: Why did god create girls?

HIM: Beats me. She acts like she wants it and then – boom – she's hysterical.

HE: Come on, man, I've watched you. You're slick – real slick – but sometimes you come on a little strong, know what I mean?

HIM: I don't think about it.

HE: Maybe you should.

HIM: Fuck it. Fuck her if she can't take a fucking joke. I don't give a fuck.

HE: Have you ever read this book?

HIM: Fuck that book.

HE: Check it out – go on, take a peek.

HIM: [GRABS BOOK AND FLIPS THROUGH IT] Holy shit. This is bad. I gotta read it. Can I have it?

HE: Well – I -- sure. I can get another copy. [HE READS OVER HIM'S SHOULDER]

SHE: All they want is to cop a feel here, grab a little there, and stick their thing anywhere it fits.

HER: I don't believe that. I can't.

SHE: He practically tried to rape you.

HER: No he didn't. He's crazy about me. He just went too far and lost control. Can't you see how much he loves me? I should be the happiest girl in the whole world. He's so cool. I love his strength, his power – I feel so small, so lost in our love. I'd do anything for that boy.

SHE: He's only a boy. Aren't you scared?

HER: Why would I be scared?

SHE: Will you – you know –

HER: Probably. How could I not? It would bring him such pleasure and make him love me more.

ABUSE ISSUES

The abuses that occur in this stage are often related to our sexuality. We may be the sexual object of a male parent or male parenting figure, such as an uncle or music teacher, or an older sibling. We may set ourselves up to be taken advantage of sexually because of the cultural expectations. By this time we abuse ourselves with cigarettes, food, alcohol, or drugs or other compulsive behaviors. We may be the objects of physical abuse by a parent who fears losing control, as we grow bigger and more independent. We may be abused by teachers, acquaintances and others who need a scapegoat. We may experience abuse and abandonment because of our parent's need to put us away in a boarding school. There are many other themes of abuse occurring in the teen years. Which the reader can no doubt supply from their own experience. The Corrective Parenting process involves the client in reliving some of the abusive experiences and in allowing themselves new and healthier experiences as if they were adolescents again.

RE-EXPERIENCING REGENERATION

SHE: What about AIDS or herpes or other junk?

HER: He'd never have any of those. Besides, this is romance – like in the movies or out of a soap opera – I won't screw it up with details. Maybe I'll take the pill. [MOVES TO SPOT] Mom, can I talk to you? Yes, Mom, I know you're there for me . . . No, I'm not in trouble . . . Mom, do you remember what you said

111

when I thought I was ready, I could ask you more about – you know – no, Mom, I'm not on drugs. But – Mom, I'm 16 years old and I'm becoming an adult. I want to take the pill . . . But you said you'd rather I take precautions than get pregnant. I want to do the right thing., now can I take the pill or not? I can always come back and ask you to help me get an abortion, Mom . . . Then help me get the pill. I'm in love and I don't what to screw it up. . . Yes, you've met him. . Right, he's the one. No, he hasn't done anything to me, Mom. He's been the perfect gentleman. A prince. Ya, he is a lot like Daddy. But I could never tell if Daddy liked me. I know he loved me, but when he – Mom, I know how you feel about it. Yes . . . Mom, listen to me – I want to take the pill. Are you gonna help me? [PULLS OFF HAT. ALA MARILYN MONROE] I have two kids and have yet to have one orgasm. It's true. I'm not frigid, just particular. I love falling in love. I've done it – oh, hundreds of time. Yes, I've even been proposed to – but I'm not ready for commitment. Thank God my mother loves my kids. Besides, I hate all that talking and figuring things out. It gets in the way of my perfecting my sexual performance. I'm good. Real fine. Just don't talk to me. Your feeling make me uncomfortable, keep them to yourself.

HIM: [MOVES INTO SPOT] Say, coach, gotta minute? . . Coach, do you ever find you can't – you know – with certain girls – No, I got no problem with my own biology and chemistry, I got that sucker down. Sometimes girls get mad at me – say I'm too aggressive . . . I remember how you said "no, no, no" always means "yes, yes, yes". But I don't know – sometimes I think "no" means "no", you know? I know she digs me – we got a thing happening between us, you know? But if I move in too close she gets hysterical. And I want her real bad . . . I know one pussy's the same as the next. But what if this is different? She's something real special . . .Priorities – of course I know my priorities [COUNTING OFF FINGERS] Drugs, sex, rock 'n roll – and of course football heads them all . . . You think those steroids'll get me into college, coach? I live for the game, Coach. I gotta do it – I don't think about nothing else . . . Ya, this girl's nothing – really Coach, I'm with you all the way. I won't let you down. [PULLS OFF HAT] There are rule-takers, rule-breakers and rule-makers. I'm a rule-maker. People want you to create rules – makes 'em feel real cozy-like. I don't even think about it. I just stroke 'em tease 'em, make them feel like my approval means everything to them. Everything. That's when I whip out my blank invoices, write up their orders, walk away with a nice looking commission. As long as they don't fuck with me, it's cool – real cool. Don't make me mad 'cause I get bad.

HE: [MOVES INTO SPOT] I couldn't help it – they stole my backpack. There was 5 grams in there. I'll pay you out of my allowance next week – I promise . . . 'Course not – I don't smoke that shit. It screws up my sinuses. Honest – see [PULLS OUT AN INHALER] This is my drug – helps me breathe . . . No, you can't see it. Look, this is the first time this has ever happened . . . Yes, it'll be the last. No, no new recruits . . . Look, I'm good at being available and invisible – but I'm no salesman . . . She? She doesn't do this shit. . All right, I'll ask . . . All right, three new customers this week. How about two? . . Okay, okay, three. Just negotiating . . . Fine, I won't . . . . Leave my parents out of this. They wouldn't believe it anyway. Besides I do this because I'm good at it – you know how I've disappeared just in the nick of time, time and time again. I'm undercover all the way. [PULLS OFF HAT] This planet is filled with scum-sucking self-centered shit for brains opportunists. There are a few visionaries, making the future safe for our children and our children's children. I work for them. I get a call, I meet a stranger who gives me something for someone somewhere. I'm good. I don't ask questions. I have half a dozen passports, a dozen identities; I have no place I have to call home. I take incredible risks. I've only killed once, but I'll never forget it because I could be next. Existence is tenuous, fragile and frail. It's not for everyone.

SHE: Doctor, can't we try another medication or another dosage? I sleep through fifth period. No, I'm not taking them – I can't function worth shit. I'll be good – I promise . . . My best friend is in love. I hate it . . .No, I'm not jealous. The guy's totally gross. Doctor, why don't I like boys? . . But I'm 16. My hormones are supposedly healthy. Are the meds doing it? . . . You don't know? How come you don't know? I miss her all the time. Am I gay? . . How do you know I'm not? I know I'm not normal. So maybe I'm a dyke. Can I tell you something? . . This is hard to say, you know? But, I like you – I think about you a lot – more than I think about anyone else. . . Transference? I don't know about any transference. Am I gay, Doctor? What should I do? If I am, I'll kill myself. It's too horrible. I'll take a razor and slash up – not across – to make sure I bleed to death. I'm a bad person, aren't I? I probably shouldn't even be alive . . . Huh? Times up so soon? [PULLS OFF HAT] I waited to tell my parents I had "come out" until I hit 30. I waited until I was upwardly mobile in my career. I waited until I bought a house. I waited until I thought I accomplished and acquired enough so that they would accept my choice. Besides, my lover was getting sick of making up stories each time she answered our phone when they'd call. They disowned me. My worst fear come to life. At least I thought it was. Actually, it was no big deal. Except – I miss them. Sometimes I feel like I still need them to validate my being.

. . .AS AN ADULT

Themes from previous stages recur in short episodes as we develop the power of regeneration. We may experience flashbacks to issues related to each previous stage creating an opportunity to reclaim our power by resolving the problems that arose during earlier stages. During regeneration we may feel lost, adrift in an uncharted land, sexually naïve and virginal. We may want to stop having sex for a while, to change partners, or to change the patterns in relationships. We may decide to be "celibate" for a while we find ourselves again. We may feel scared or angry as we seek ways to integrate our sexual desires with our much "younger" needs for nurturing and support. We may expect to come out of this process relating to the world in a new and grownup way, having moved beyond the relationships that once were our mainstay for support. If we reach adulthood with unfinished adolescent business, we may be rebellious and play sexual games. We may be self-centered and vengeful, lack intimacy in relationships, uncomfortable in situations where we are required to establish close warm relationships. We may have unfinished dependency needs, be very competitive and play games such as "one-upmanship" (mine is better than yours) to get our need for strokes met.

NEGATIVE REGENERATION MESSAGES

[THE FOLLOWING SPEECHES ARE SAID IN-DIVIDUALLY AND THEN CHANTED TO-GETHER FOUR TIMES AS ACTORS SPEAK TO DIFFERENT PARTS OF THE AUDIENCE]

SHE: There's not enough, why should there be. It's silly to even ask.

HE: Existence is tenuous, fragile and frail. It's not for everyone.

HIM: Don't make me mad 'cause I get bad. Don't make me mad 'cause I get bad.

HER: Your feelings make me uncomfortable. Keep them to yourself.

[MUSIC. ALL DANCE. THEY DANCE TO-GETHER, DANCE APART, STEAL EACH OTH-ER'S PARTNERS, ETC.]

POSITIVE REGENERATION MESSAGES

ALL: Script rewrite! Even if we don't know how, we were put on this planet to regenerate and procreate.

[THEY MAKE SOUNDS AND MOVEMENTS TO ACCOMPANY A RAP]

We got sexuality
And we're here to say
Redoing stages of ages

And we're here to stay
We're gonna be just like you
We'll do the way you do
You taught us everything we know
We're adults – like you

HE: We are?

SHE: Our show

HER: Can we do it?

HIM: Who knows?

HE: I want the world to see me

SHE: There's a place for me I know

HER: I love to learn and learn to love

HIM: I let my feelings show

HIM/HER: Hey baby can do it
In a safe and sexy way

HE/SHE: We know we can be friendly
Thoughts of sex are far away

HIM/HER: You don't?

HE/SHE: Don't want it
Do you?

HIM/HER: We do it

ALL: Be in be out
Be over under through

Mistake to learn
Learn to mistake
We got sexuality
And we're here to say
Redoing stages of ages
And we're here to stay

We are?
Our show
We can do it?
Who knows?
Hmph

HEALING RITUALS

Psychodramas are especially useful for the grownup with adolescent business to finish. Regression to the teen years or earlier years where problems originated allows a client to get good parental support for developmental tasks such as setting limits and developing a healthy sexuality. Assignments to observe and model healthy teenagers, to participate in healthy teen type activities, to learn to set limits on one's behavior, and to incorporate appropriate self-care beliefs for this stage are useful healing rituals. Another ritual includes having slumber parties with other clients who are challenging some of their dysfunctional beliefs at this stage, with parenting figure who will be there to be responsive, and set appropriate parenting limits. For men, who lacked an appropriate male figure when they were kids, being taught how to shave can be useful. For women, learning how to use make-up from a caring adult is healing. The number of rituals for this stage is limited only by the imagination and creativity of the participants.

CASE STUDY

A forty-five-year-old woman was experiencing the transition of divorce. She had led a sheltered life as a child. As an adolescent she went to a Catholic girl's school and had gone from high school to the convent where she lived as a nun for the next twenty years. She had left the convent to marry an ex-priest. In therapy, she was aware that her experiences with sexuality and sensuality were extremely limited. Stories of the dangers and disgusts of sex had been used to frighten her. She still carried some of these. She contracted to study the healthy adolescents whom she knew, and to do regressive work to the teen years with the therapist as a healthy parent. In-group she got appropriate parental advice and the necessary limit-setting from her therapist/mom towards becoming fully healthy sexual adult. In doing this work she realized that she needed to so some younger work as three or four-year-old, which she did in conjunction with the adolescent work. As she did the work, she found herself feeling more confident in relationships within her group. She began to be more fully understanding of her sexual self, and started going out on an occasional date.

CONCLUSION

Corrective Parenting and Rechilding start with the premise common to most modern psychotherapy models – that adult dysfunctions arise from traumatic childhood experiences. It carries the healing process a step further than merely identifying by releasing the energy from the childhood traumas. People working in the model recreate new healthy childhood memories and experiences that replace the unhealthy ones under which they have been living. They do so by using the metaphors and rituals denoted by "being little", "Rechilding", and creating "new parent messages" which are affirming and empowering. People experiencing a recycling of earlier stages often are confused by the fact that they can be recycling two or more different stages at the same time as the flashbacks they experience take them back to more than one early set of feelings, thoughts and sensations. It is important that the therapist understands this fact.

The Corrective Parenting and Rechilding model is relatively new. It is largely derived from Transactional Analysis and Reparenting models, and has been in practice for approximately thirty five years in a number of centers across the United States, Canada, Europe, Australia and India. The cornerstone of the Corrective Parenting/Rechilding model is the parenting contract. It requires a complete commitment by the therapist to be there for the client no matter what he experiences, exactly as a healthy parent would do. The contract requires openness and risk-taking on the part of the "new parent" beyond what is usual in a therapist-client relationship, both to support the client's process, and to model healthy behavior. This is a very personal contracted commitment the key tool through which the model works. The therapist must also be committed to working through their own "counter-transference" issues with their own therapist so they do not repeat for the client, the unhealthy parenting of their own and the client's past. It is not wise to undertake working in this model with someone who is not committed in this way, nor is it wise to make such an undertaking without a clear understanding of what it entails. It is not a simple process.

Grieving each stage of life is a meticulous and demanding task.

You, the reader, may judge the model for yourself on the basis of whether it speaks to your inner part, and whether you identify with any part of it or not.

You can trust your inner wisdom.

Corrective Parenting is one of many paths to health and personal growth and must be chosen with care as to whether it is to be yours. It is not true that nothing can be done about child abuse. First it can be prevented, and second, it can be and is healed every day. It is important to heal the old wounds and not to ignore them. Ignoring them leads to dysfunctional behaviors and ill health. Should you identify what we have shared with you here in this book, and if you are willing and have the courage to take the risk and commit yourself to your health, that dear little child that is within, and to learning how to take care of yourself in appropriate ways, it could be a process full of growth and joy.

IT'S NEVER TOO LATE TO HAVE A HAPPY CHILDHOOD!

BIBLIOGRAPHY

Boyd, L. and Boyd H., "Blocking Tragic Scripts", <u>Transactional 1980a Analysis Journal</u>, 1980, Vol. 10, pp 227-230.

Boyd, L. and Boyd H., "Going Crazy", <u>Transactional Analysis Journal</u>, 1980. Vol. 10, pp 317-320.

Childs-Gowell, Elaine, <u>Are you Grieving?</u>, self-published, 1988, Seattle, Washington.

Childs-Gowell, Elaine, <u>Reparenting Schizophrenics: The 1979 Cathexis Experience</u>, Christopher House, 1979, Boston Massachusetts.

Childs-Gowell, Elaine, <u>Bodyscript Blockbusting</u>, Murray Publishing, 1978, Seattle, Washington.

Childs-Gowell, Elaine, <u>The Cathexis Primer</u>, Murray Publishing, 1979, Seattle, Washington.

Clarke, Jean I., Self-Esteem A Family Affair, Winston Press, 1981, Minneapolis, Minnesota.

Clarke, Jean I., <u>Help! Books For Parents</u>, Harper and Row, 1986, San Francisco, California.

Emerson, W., Presentation at Pre and Perinatal Psychology Association, June 1987, San Francisco, California.

Farrant, G., Keynote address at Pre and Perinatal Psychology Association, June 1987, San Francisco, California.

Findheisen, B., <u>Journey to be Born</u>, (video), produced by Star Foundation, 1987.

Grof, S., <u>Realms of the Human Unconscious</u>, Viking Press, 1975, New York, New York.

Holloway, W., <u>Shut the Escape Hatch</u>, Monograph IV, Holloway Publishers, 1973.

Houston, Jean. Address at workshop, 1984, Seattle, Washington.

Janov, A., <u>Imprints: The Life-long Effects of the Birth Experience</u>, Coward McCann, 1983, New York, New York.

Landsman, Sandra, <u>Found! A Place for Me</u>, Treehouse Enterprises, 1984, Farmington Hills, Michigan.

Landsman Sandra, <u>I'm Special</u>, Treehouse Enterprises, 1986, Farmington Hills, Michigan.

Levin, Pamela, <u>Becoming the Way We Are</u>, self-published, 1974, Ukiah, California.

Levin, Pamela, <u>Cycles of Power</u>, self-published, 1980, Ukiah, California.

Miller, Alice, <u>The Drama of the Gifted Child</u>, Harper and Rowe, 1983, New York, New York.

Miller, Alice, <u>For Your Own Good: Hidden Cruelty in Childrearing and the Roots of Violence</u>, Farrar, Strauss, Giroux, 1983, New York, New York.

Miller, Alice, <u>Thou Shalt Not Be Aware: Society's Betrayal of the Child</u>, Farrar, Strauss, Giroux, 1983. New York, New York.

Schiff, Jacqui and Beth Day, <u>All My Children</u>, J.B. Lippencott, 1970, New York, New York.

Schiff, Jacqui, et al, <u>The Cathexis Reader</u>, Harper and Row, 1975, New York, New York.

Whitfield, C., <u>Healing the Child Within</u>, Health Communications, Inc., 1987. Pompano Beach, Florida.

GLOSSARY

aggregation: the resulting change in attitude and perception of one's usual way of being after a ritual.

agitation: not paying attention to feelings and instead putting the energy into physical discomfort or in repetitive non-problem solving behavior, such as hand wringing, pacing, cleaning the house when the house is not the problem.

appropriate: that which is socially acceptable in a particular situation.

Aquagenesis: conducted in a warm pool or tub to assist client recycle gaps in development.

archaic parent: antiquated and unhealthy internalized parent.

"be little": regress to an early age

caring: mattering to one another

cathexis: the shifting and concentration of energy in a part of your personality: as in "cathect Adult".

check-out: concluding exercise in a healing ritual process to have taken place in a weekly therapy group or marathon where clients express feelings and thoughts about their experience and review contracts.

co-dependent: addictive and dysfunctional behaviors in relationships, often resulting in symbiosis.

competition: setting up WIN/LOSE situation with another person

confrontation: caring:. Telling someone you are uncomfortable with what they are doing or saying.

contract: a set of agreements made between the client and the therapist and or group for specific pieces of therapeutic work. Also used for goal setting, and protection.

corner contract: client moves to a quiet place to think through inappropriate behavior, often resulting from breaking one of the self-care contracts.

corrective parenting: giving up old dysfunctional Parent and inappropriate belief systems. Usually done on an outpatient basis by contract for short periods of time. (see Reparenting).

counter-transference: interfering phenomenon in which psychiatrist or psychotherapist views client as child or love object.

dealing: taking responsibility for your behavior by relating to the situation, the feelings and the issues.

denial: see discounting, below.

discounting: not taking responsibility for or not relating to part or all of what is going on here and now. Not being aware of the situation, the feelings, and the issues. Ignoring, minimizing or aggrandizing aspects of self and other's thoughts, feelings, wants and needs and problem-solving ability.

doing nothing: you do nothing relevant to solving a particular or specific problem

ego boundaries: an understanding where one's needs, wants, feelings and issues end and another's begins.

ego states: Parent, Adult, Child are parts of the personality which we use for transacting with other people.

escalation: non-thinking building up feelings until the person explodes in verbal or physical violence. A person escalates in order to avoid dealing or taking responsibility for what is going on here and now. Not caring, and not being aware of the situation, the feelings, the issues. (see Passive Behaviors, below).

frame-of-reference: the way each individual person views the world.

gestalt: perceiving the whole rather than the sum of the parts.

incapatation: non-thinking, pulling inward and shutting off all outside input. Non-thinking shutting off of feelings, sometimes done with alcohol, food or drugs and/or depression.

injunction: a parental command internalized as truth or appropriate.

intensification rituals: rituals used to magnify feelings such as: rage restraints, pillow beatings, towel pulling, etc.

intrusion ritual: an intervention where the client tries to shut out all input and stimuli as the therapist intrude with messages like "this baby won't die", or "I want this baby to live," etc.

issues: problem areas which may include individual problems, developmental issues or gaps, areas of socialization such as obsessive-compulsive behaviors, caring for self or others, etc.

limen: the altered state resulting from moving into the experiential part of a ritual, also called threshold.

metaphor: a word, phrase or image used to describe another word, phrase or image.

mistaken belief system: the belief system on which a script is built. Similar to frame-of-reference, core belief.

over adaptation: a person does things only because they believe someone else wants them to.

paradigm: pattern, example or model

parenting: appropriate and healthy care taking and information giving.

perinatal: stage of development during birth.

pons stimulation procedure: lightly rubbing slapping and deeply massaging the client's arms and legs.

prenatal: stage of development before birth.

psychodrama: scenarios that replay past experiences.

rage restraint: an intensification healing ritual where client pushes with body and voice against the five or more people holding them safely to the mat while relating anger-triggering messages to help client release angry energy around specific injunctions.

reactive: acting on one's response to a circumstance or person through confrontation or an appropriate emotional reaction.

recycling: re-experiencing feelings, thoughts and experience from early developmental stages.

redefining: responding to only part of what is going on and changing the meaning to fit your own mistaken belief system.

regression: being Little and relating only from the Child. The Parent and Adult are excluded or set aside momentarily. When this is done appropriately, there is a contract to do so before hand.

Reichian breathing: a controlled breathing technique used in conjunction with guided imagery to assist client recycle gaps in development.

reparenting: giving up the old destructive Parent and establishing a new Parent that incorporates healthy and appropriate Parent information and actions. Similar to Corrective Parenting except that the setting is usually in-patient.

resistance: survival mechanisms learned early in life that become ways of sabotaging and resisting a move or change towards a healthy way of being.

respond: to relate to what is going on here and now., i.e. to be responsive vs. passive.

ritual: a formal ceremonial system and procedure moving participants through three stages.

script: that set of mistaken beliefs and decisions made when the person was too young to have clear information about the reality of the larger world.

seductive behavior: when a person acts as though they need something or tries to get somebody to do something for them while avoiding being direct about it.

separation: a way of segregating the ritual participant from their usual way of being.

shifting energy: avoiding thinking, feeling, or doing something about a problem and setting things up for the other person to experience your discomfort.

strokes: message (positive or negative) that reinforce a state of being or a way of behaving.

symbiosis: co-dependent attachment to another where ego boundaries are not identified.

threshold: the altered state resulting from moving into the experiential part of a ritual, also called limen.

transference: a phenomenon in which the client adopts the psychiatrist or psychotherapist as a parent.

REGRESSION
and PROTECTION

PART I: STANDARDS OF PRACTICE IN REGRESSION
AND CORRECTIVE PARENTING THERAPIES

PART II: CONTRACTING FOR SELF-CARE

PART III: BUDDHA'S MIDDLE WAY AND CORRECTIVE
PARENTING'S MIDDLE GROUND

*Protection for both therapist
and clients in the creation of
"healing rituals" in psychotherapy
when dealing with deep shock and
trauma in clients.*

Elaine Childs Gowell, PhD

Private Practice Psychosocial Nursing
4702 Aurora Av. N. Seattle.Wa.98103

Contents

PART II:

PART III

SUMMARY:

REGRESSION AND PROTECTION: STANDARDS OF PRACTICE FOR REGRESSIVE THERAPIES AND CORRECTIVE PARENTING.

These pages outline the Standards of Practice created by a group of psychotherapists who have undertaken to revise the Reparenting and Re-childing Model of psychotherapy known as Corrective Parenting to fit the therapy of clients who are outpatient, who have therapy once or twice a week and have need to be maintaining their lives in society. These standards are devised to provide guidelines for the therapists and the clients who are using some of the more intensive forms of therapy such as Body Work, Bioenergetics, Parenting Contracts, and Regression to childhood issues. These guidelines provide definitions, minimum conditions, recommended conditions and descriptions of various procedures or "rituals" for the practice of Corrective Parenting. Definitions, rationale and philosophical considerations are discussed. The structure of the procedures "healing rituals" are carefully delineated in terms of protection for both clients and therapists.

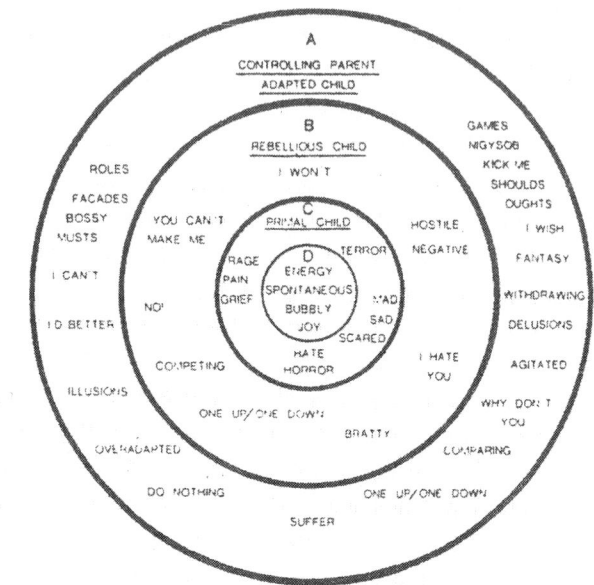

Layered view of the personality, showing script issues to be worked through in treatment.

INTRODUCTION:

The purpose of this publication is to present a model for Standards of Practice for use in Regressive Work and Corrective Parenting with clients. This is especially significant because in these ways of working there are different risks and vulnerabilities. Since the early seventies a rich and powerful group process has evolved centering on a developmental model of the Self. Corrective Parenting is a positive transference therapeutic model in which the therapist uses him or herself in what Sullivan and Peplau defined as the "Therapeutic use of Self" (1964). The therapist does this to provide the support and structure for certain clients who have long needed to challenge very deep and very young core issues of trauma and shock. The original reparenting model (Schiff 1971) has continued to add to its structure and to expand with the theoretical contributions of the Experiencing Enough staff, (Pam Levin, Jean Illsey Clarke, Filepe Garcia, Gail Nordeman, Elaine Childs-Gowell, et al 1974,1982, 1988, 1993). Others who's theoretical structures have contributed are Sandra Landsman(1984) William Emerson(1987) Elizabeth Marcher (1992), Peter Levine (1993), Stanislas Grof (1985), Past Life Therapies (Lucas et al 1995), which are considered to also be regression therapies, and many others. It is understood that where unusual and "cutting edge" methods are being used it is imperative that the therapists have some guidelines for their practice, therefore a group of these psychotherapists whose backgrounds included the disciplines of psychology, nursing, social work, anthropology and counseling came together and created the Standards of Practice as outlined below.

RATIONALE FOR REGRESSIVE WORK:

During this author's studies in Anthropology it became evident that it is in the altered state of consciousness (ASC) that the deepest healing occurs. Having also observed that some of these altered states vary in intensity and depth , it was noted that often the individual does not accept that they have even experienced an altered state, as in Ericksonian Hypnosis (Erickson: 1980). At other times, the subject is aware of having "traveled" to other times and places and has a vivid recollection of this "journey". This other time and place is often a childhood experience which affects the rational adult being in the here and now world. These altered states may also be observed as dissociative disorders. If we as therapist/healers are to provide for the clients a true shift in consciousness towards their healing, we must be able to assist them in achieving the shift in psychic energy which brings about a "cure", or as Berne called, "removal of the splinter" (Berne: 1961). Many of the techniques, procedures, or if you will, "Rituals" (van der Hart 1978;Childs-Gowell:1979), involve the participant(s) in activities which induce the altered state of consciousness during which the healing occurs. As clinicians and as students of Transactional Analysis it is evident to us that the ability to cathect energy from one ego state to another is impaired in many of our clients. They seem to get "stuck" in some aspect of their Child Ego State, or Parent Ego State, and often have difficulty in the cathexis of their Adult Ego State. This condition causes great dis-ease and is relieved by the release of the "bound energy" in that particular Ego State. If there is no structure for the release of energy the person may repeat archaic experiences over and over again, retraumatize themselves, becoming "stuck" in their dysfunctional behaviors. They will thus deepen the shock and traumas experienced earlier in life when the unhealthy or faulty "decision" was made. Over the years there have been many therapies devised which have created "procedures", ie "Rituals" to provide the client with the release of the bound energy. Examples include, Reichian (Reich:1972), Redecision (Goulding: 1972), and Gestalt (Perls: 1969). It has become evident that while these therapies are generally effective with the post-verbal client, Corrective Parenting interventions were developed for those clients whose archaic traumas are in the main, pre-verbal. Recognizing the need for clinicians to provide 1) protection for the clients in the enacting of aspects of preverbal therapies, in particular the bonding and attachment disorders it was deemed necessary to provide them with 2) a structure to empower them to create a new channel for the bound energy; 3) the permission to procede with the regressive piece of work, a set of guidelines needed to be provided so that both therapists and clients would be able to procede in a safe manner. The Inner-Child-of-the-Past is released from the archaic Script Decisions, and False Beliefs. Corrective Parenting and Rechilding (Childs-Gowell : 1976), were the result of the author's choice to limit the parenting role of the therapist to the treatment room in contrast to Reparenting (Schiff 1972) where the therapist takes on the constant role of parent both inside and outside of the sessions.

PHILOSOPHICAL CONSIDERATIONS

Many people seeking Corrective Parenting and Regressive therapies have had many other therapists, mostly "talk" therapy,and have found themselves frustrated, because their deep "somatic shock and trauma" issues have not been addressed. Or, as in the case of some of the body therapies, they have experienced being re-traumatized. Along with these deep issues are often those issues of attachment disorder and spiritual issues where the client feels trapped in their dis-ease, and separate from Self. Clients find that by bonding with the therapist in their therapeutic process they are able to clear up their deep somatic and archaic work, and are better able to experience their spiritual source. The release of the pain from these earlier issues creates an opening to higher consciousness, and often sets people on the path of spiritual understanding which they believe they lost in the struggle and suffering of their dis-ease. "By crossing, in ecstasy, the dangerous bridge" (Eliade:1969) that connects the ordinary from the non-ordinary, this bridge which only the dead, and those who learn to "die while living" through meditation practices, can attempt, the client proves that he or she is spirit, and more simply a "human being on a spiritual path". (Theihard de Chardin: 1965). There is evidence to support the belief that therapists are the shamans/spiritual guides of the modern urban age. Therapeutic rituals bring about changes not only in symbolic ways, but also in many other ways. Ono van der Hart (1979) says ^If a ritual is prescribed......the clients can experience the performing of the ritual as a meaningful pursuit; a task through which they can get rid of ....." their dis-ease.(pp.192-193)

> The sun sets and the moon sets,
> But they are not gone. Death
> Is a coming together.
> The tomb looks like a prison,
> but it's reallly release
> into Union.   Rumi

DEFINITIONS AND PROCESSES:

In the process of exploring the possibility of creating a discipline under the rubric of Corrective Parenting, a group of the clinicians involved came up with following definitions to describe the processes and minimum expectations for safety, protection and permission requisite to provide an ethical and safe program for clients. The name Corrective Parenting was originally coined by Brenda Schaeffer (1983) with the publication of the developmental chart by the same name. It is with her permission in 1990 that the group of therapists in Seattle in the late 1970's decided to use it to describe a form of regressive psychotherapy based on Transactional Analysis (Berne:1964ff) Reparenting (Schiff et al 1975ff), Reichian (Reich: 1958ff), Adlerian (Adler:1932), Gestalt (Perls: 1976a, 1976b), Sullivanian (Sullivan:1955) , Redecision (Goulding:1972), Self Reparenting (James: 1976), and Psychodrama (Moreno: 1959).

A CORRECTIVE PARENTING GROUP:

A group where regressive work is done is a therapy group lead by a licensed or certified therapist or counselor who has had extensive training in Corrective Parenting. This training includes a minimum of three years of personal experience in Regressive therapies or a Corrective Parenting group as a client themselves, and at least six months experience in assisting in groups and therapeutic marathons (ie weekend intensive sessions). The group will meet weekly for a minmum of two to two and a half hours. There will be a procedure for checking into group such as writing agendae or contracts for the day on the board, announcements and brags, and a group meditation, lesson, or exercise to focus group energy. The group will proceed on the basis of the agendae, and will end with a closing where each person checks-in to ascertain that Adult Ego States are cathected, the work is anchored, and everyone is then safe to go home.

ETHICAL GUIDELINES:

Definition: Specific values that are applied to the practice of Corrective Parenting psychotherapy.

Minimum Conditions: a) Each therapist will subscribe to the ethics code of their own particular professional organization (psychology, nursing, counseling, medicine, education, ITAA etc.) b) Each therapist using these procedures will subscribe to these recommended standards of practice. c) The commitment by the therapist to these standards will be made known to the client in writing, at the beginning of their therapy. d) the therapist realizes that because of the bonding and attachment disorders of their clients they are making a long term (five to ten years) commitment to the client. The therapist who does not abide by these guidelines, and those of their state licensing division will be reported to their professional organization and to the state authority under which they are practicing.

THE GROUP THERAPY CONTRACT:

Definition: A signed agreement between the client and therapist(s) made before the client joins the group.

The minimum conditions: a) the client signs the contract prior to the first group session and keeps a copy of the contract. b) the contract includes: (1) the Self Care agreements, confidentiality, physical safety at the location of therapy group (for liability reasons), (2) the understanding that the group members and therapists abstain from the use of alcohol at least 24 hours prior to group, (3) that the client or therapist will not use illegal drugs or indulge in self-medication with alcohol at any time during their therapy contract, (4) a structure for leaving group is provided and understood, (5) fee and payment agreements are clearly stated. Further, it is recommended that the a. contracts be reviewed periodically, b. the therapist adapts the contract(s) to their own and the client's situation.

PERSONAL THERAPY CONTRACTS:

Definition: Agreements the clients make with themselves, therapists and group members, to guide their therapy process and keep them safe. Contracts will be focused on the client's own goals, and on the elimination of ineffective behaviors or life decisions that the client wishes to change and on the creation of effective behaviors and new and more effective life decisions.

Minimum conditions: a) all clients and therapists will agree to keep the Self Care Contracts, which are based on the theoretical information on closing escape hatches (Holloway: 1973) (Boyd:1980a,1980b) (the Experiencing Enough Staff: Gowell, Levin, Garcia, Nordeman, Clarke). These Self Care Contracts are as follows:

1. I do not kill, or harm myself or others, nor do I provoke others to harm me, accidentally or on purpose. I stay safe and respectful, and alive.

2. I do not run away, physically or emotionally, or engage in running behaviors. I stay and work through the problem.

3. I do not go crazy or make myself sick to avoid problems. I stay sane and healthy.

4. I am not sneaky nor do I lie or steal. I am honest and congruent in my thoughts and feelings.

5. I am not passive. I am proactive, and confront passivity in myself and others, and accept their confrontation of my passivity. (Reactivity: Garcia:1995)

6. I do not regress without a contract. I set structure before regressing.

7. I am responsible for my thoughts, feelings and actions to others and to myself.

   a) All clients will review and update their contracts periodically.
   b)Contracts must be clear, specific and measurable.

Recommended conditions: a) A new client may rely on the self-care contracts to increase personal awareness and develop other individual contracts as they progress in their therapy. b) Clients will be accountable for breaking their contracts and will do accountability work (see definition below) on broken contracts. c) Therapists may suggest additional complimentary self care contracts as needed.

PARENTING CONTRACTS:

Definition: A Parenting contract is one which makes explicit the positive transference that has occurred and how the therapist is to act as a "new and healthy therapeutic Parent" to the client's Child. Through this process the client has the opportunity to arrange for, and experience healthy ways of bonding, attachment , connecting and growing while in therapy.

Minimum conditions: a) the client has a good foundation in keeping the Self Care Contracts and the ability to cathect Adult Ego State when required. b) The contract is never assumed and must be invoked for each piece of regressive therapy. c) The contract is initiated by the client, and agreed upon by the therapist and the group. d) The therapist is prepared to maintain this contract in the face of negative transference from the client, personal life changes, and crises, renegotiating the contract when necessary. The client agrees to maintain the contract in the face of negative transference, and as long as the contract serves its purpose.

Minimum conditions The parenting contract is a part of the individual's therapeutic process, and the individual's work, and is not essential for all clients. a) When the client leaves therapy for any reason, the status of the parenting contract is clarified, and terminated, or made accessible as determined by each individual client and their therapist. b) The contract must be negotiated, clarified, and agreed upon in the group setting, and supported by the group. c)The contract is entered into the therapy contract book maintained for each group. d) the contract is to be used by the client only when they contract in the moment for parenting,(ie in group, in a private session, or during a telephone session), and in group only if written on the group agenda. e) A parenting contract is honored by other therapists and not co-opted without consultation with the other therapist and the client. f)The parenting contract must be developmentally appropriate at all times. This means that during therapy the therapist will empower the client by simultaneously respecting that the client is an adult. The therapist will treat the client as a child only during contracted regression work g) If the client has not completed the contracted developmental rechilding work, (i.e. still has developmental gaps to be addressed) and leaves group, the option of the parenting contract may be maintained by mutual agreement as a resource to the client. h) the ethical position of "once a parent, always a parent" is a part of the therapist's consciousness even after the ending of a parenting contract, in the same sense in which one remains the parent of grown up biological children. i) On-going parenting contracts are negotiated only as an aspect of the adult relationship of the client and former therapist. j) It is recommended that the ethical position of "once a client always a client" be maintained indefinitely because clients may need to return to therapy in the future as new issues arise, and as old issues recycle.

> You can't prevent birds of sorrow
> flying over your head - but you
> can prevent them from building
> nests in your hair.
> Ancient Chinese Proverb

ACCOUNTABILITY WORK:

(AKA: The Corner, Time Out, The Think Chair, West Work(the West in the Medicine Wheel being the place of Integrity: Villoldo: 1988); (Corner: Schiff et al 1975).

Definition: This work is designed to encourage the client to address the Script behaviors which are self-defeating. It invites the client to think about their aberrant, self-harming, or anti-social behaviors. It is drawn from the Reparenting Model (Schiff et al 1975) from Adlerian contracting (Adler 1953) and encounter work. This process, when used appropriately, (ie cognitively) provides a structure in which the client can connect thoughts, feelings and underlying psychological issues with the behavior patterns that have resulted in their breaking a Self Care Contract.

Recommended Conditions: a) There must be a set of agreements or contracts known in advance to the client to which he or she may refer; b) the client agrees to be the accountable i.e. when they break contracts or on the rare occasion when clients are confronted about doing their accountability work (as opposed to confronting themselves), c) two or more group members must be in agreement on the necessity of this process for the client.

Minimum conditions: a) there is a procedure in place for the client to check out their thinking when they are complete, b) the client has op-

143

portunity for assistance when needed c)a process which they can use to aid them in their thinking about the issues, (there is a protocol for this), they can ask for coaching. d) an agreement is made that the client will reasonably and authentically address the problem and not over adapt to the group. e) Accountability work must NOT be used punitively, assigned to resolve a conflict, or used by the client or therapist inappropriately (i.e. to abuse self, to isolate, to create conflict , to engage in a power struggle etc.)

Further Recommendations: a)For new clients, less than three months in group, the accountability work and review of the thinking must be done in group; b) Initially and as needed the client may have a coach and c) the client separates from but is not isolated from the group while doing the work, so that they may be encouraged to think about their own process and not be distracted by the ongoing group process. d) after three months in group, clients are encouraged to do their thinking and their checkouts outside of group, and report in to the group on their process.

GAME GROUP, NEGATIVE AND POSITIVE STROKE CIRCLES:

Definition: These are interventions whereby the client(s) may give and receive the Brown Stamps (Berne: 1964) also known as Negative Strokes they are in need of to keep from playing Games out in the world, or as in the case of the Positive stroke circle, they receive the positive strokes they need to keep their stroke economy banks filled (Steiner: 1971). The theoretical issues behind these interventions have to do with giving the client an arena in which they can externalize the Critical Parent and get rid of their own Negative Self-Talk, and hear good things about themselves.

Minimum conditions: a) the client(s) contract for these procedures; b) the client(s) has enough active Adult to be able to learn from the experience. c) the therapist(s) are peers during the Game d) there is always a debriefing period and client(s) are expected to do "work" on issues which have become a problem as a result of the Game. e) there is a period of nurture following the Game. f) the Game is not to be offered by a therapist who has not had personal experience of this process. g) the therapist is also responsible for dealing with their own process outside of group, if the procedure "hooked" them.

The Negative Stroke Circle gives the client(s) an opportunity to hear from others the "negative self talk" which is their own, the purpose being to externalize the Critical Parent.

Minimum conditions: a)the client will contract for at least three sessions over a three week period. The client does not rebut. b) the session will last between 3 and 5 minutes. c) the client will debrief after the process. d) the client contracts for an advocate during the process, e)the client will be nurtured following a negative stroke circle. f) the participating clients will be aware of the process and be focused, and debrief their own learning from the experience.

The Positive Stroke Circle gives the client(s) the opportunity to hear positive statements about themselves in a concentrated and time limited manner . The positive stroke circle lasts 3-5 minutes and the receiver simply listens and says "thank you". There are no rebuttals. Those who have difficulty accepting good statements about themselves will find even more trying than the negative stroke circle.

Minimum conditions: a) the client will contract for the process b) the session will last no longer than five minutes c) the client will debrief after the process.

The Game Group: This process is done once a month or by group concensus. In it the participants have an opportunity to practice the "Games" they are familiar with in life, or to learn and practice the other games (Berne:1964). The Redefining Hexagon (Mellor:1975b) is used as a basis for this process.

Recommended processes: a)the Game Group be time-limited, and the time agreed upon before it starts. b)the clients offer script beliefs and issues to be gamed upon. c) the client who is particularly vulnerable at the time such as recently bereaved, or in the midst of challenging very young issues in their process, does not participate. d) the client who cannot maintain Adult Ego State does not participate. e)new clients have the opportunity to observe a Game Group at least once before participating. f) Game Group be offered regularly each month and the length of the game be voted upon by the group, g) a client may call for Game Group at any time as a part of their agenda. h) the right to not participate at any particular time may be negotiated.

THERAPEUTIC HOLDING/ NURTURING/TOUCHING:

Definition: The practice of a practitioner or group member physically holding or touching another person, while under contract. There is no touching, holding or nurturing without mutual consent. The purpose is for positive stroking and also for participants to differentiate between nurturing touch and sexual touch.

Minimum conditions: a) the client will contract for this procedure; b) The client(s) will be given information that all touching will be non-sexual and is completely voluntary for both parties. c) The client must have the ability to and have the commitment to stop the holding, or touching, to clear up any misunderstanding, misperception, redefinition or concerns that the client may have or which may arise as they receive or later give touching or nurturing. c) both the holdee/ touchee and the holder/ toucher are clear that the holding/touching is nurturing, and not sexual.

Recommended processes: a) holding/ touching occurs, only in the group setting, b) if holding is to occur in individual sessions then it only when the client is or has been in a group so that the understanding is clear that this is for nurture only. c) When holding a client, the therapist ensures that the client is not holding him or herself up or "taking care of" the holder. d) For clients with histories of incest, dissociative disorders, borderline personality, histrionic, and thought disorders, special sensitivity to establishing a clearly defined structure is imperative. e) the client's demonstrated ability to refrain from spontaneous regression is expected and required. f) the therapist is clear that they are not doing this to get their own needs met, and it is clear to both therapist and client that it is a therapeutic intervention. g)Holding and touching in nurturing ways is designed to be a therapeutic intervention. h) Sex with a client is NEVER therapeutic, and even sexual energy can cause damage to a regressed client. i) If the therapist has boundary problems they should not engage in this process. j)Therapists are not to engage in parenting when there is no parenting contract (positive transference) this is to be made explicit and clients are aware of this fact. k) it is recommended that therapist not "hold" a client in individual sessions where there are no witnesses to the process.

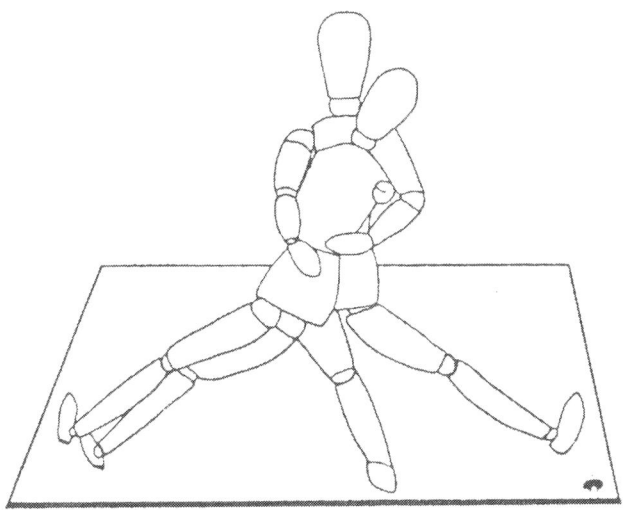

Holding: Nurturing and being nurtured.

REGRESSION WORK:

Definition: Regression work is a process in which the client selects a specific age within which to work and assumes the altered state of consciousness requisite for the age. Regression work for the purpose of working through archaic traumas and filling in developmental gaps, may occur at any age from preconception through age 19 years.

Minimum conditions: a) a client must be able to maintain conscious awareness of ordinary reality (i.e. their observing self is present). b) A therapist must be present to supervise the regression and/ or provide the contracted for "healthy parenting". c) The therapist must have knowledge of developmental theory and have experience in facilitating regression work. d) The client must be able to cathect Adult and function adequately in adult awareness before leaving the therapeutic setting.

Recommended processes: a) When a client regresses spontaneously, the therapist will focus primarily on returning the client to Adult functioning in order to empower the client to set up the piece of work with appropriate structure, as opposed to encouraging further regression without a contract. b) The client and the therapist will be aware of the client's goal for doing the regression work, and the client must be able to state this. If the work is to fill in developmental gaps, the client will commit to having a new experience and to making new and positive decisions. c) Generally, regression work will not be done prior to the client or the therapist leaving on vacation, or immediately prior to the client leaving therapy.

> Autonomy is manifested by the release or
> Recovery of three capacities: awareness,
> Spontanaeity, and intimacy.   Eric Berne

PONS, DEEP MASSAGE, SENSORY STIMULATION TECHNIQUES:

Definition: Contracted processes requested by the client for the purpose of lessening the client's physical withdrawal and isolation, and dissociative states. These processes stimulate the deep neural networks which the client may have shut down as a protective measure in their archaic experience of abuse. The pons stimulation involves the client and two or more persons who starting with their hands on the client's head offer a deep massage, against the bone of each body part descending to the feet and stating the body part as they move their hands (i.e. "this is your arm, chest, thigh etc") this is followed by light tapping with cupped hands, and ends with sweeping the person's aura. Sensory stimulation such as tapping the body with finger tips, or slapping the bottoms of the feet may be included, to stimulate the cerebellum and pons.

Minimum conditions: a). The procedure is conducted in the group setting. b) The client agrees to experience feelings and report on thoughts which arise from the procedure. c) The touch on the part of the therapist(s) and or group members is deep and firm, and provides sensory stimulation as the procedure defines.

Recommended processes: a) The therapist be well schooled in using such techniques. b) Therapists with nursing, massage therapy, social work, and medical backgrounds are advised to review their State laws concerning their Scope of Practice. Others such as psychologists, and counsellors need to be aware of the limitations to touch advised by the State laws under which they are licensed to practice.

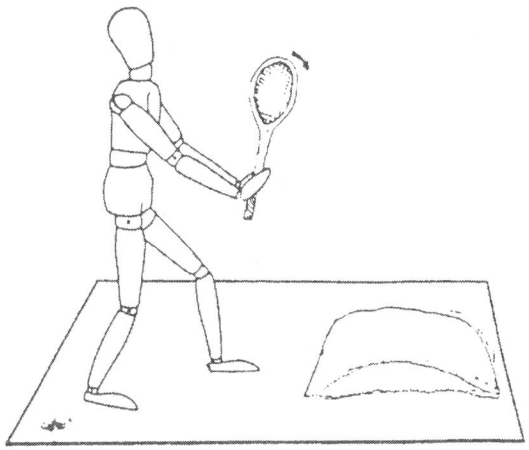

SOFT AND HARD INTRUSION/ BOUNDARING WORK:

Definition: Contracted procedures may be initiated as requested by the client. In this process, the therapist or group may physically or verbally intrude on the client in a manner which is socially seen as intrusive. Soft intrusion is gentle and sometimes unexpected attention which may or may not include touching, hands, head etc. Examples are described above under Pons, massage etc. Soft intrusion may also include eye contact, verbal acknowledging, light touch on appropriate body parts, hugs, hand holding, verbal strokes of a large variety. Hard intrusion may involve the client in a physical restraint, utilization of pressure points, eye contact used to interrupt a client's pattern of deep withdrawal and isolation.

Minimum conditions: a) Hard intrusion is a client-contracted procedure which is undertaken only with a clear contract, only in groups, marathons or minithons and only in the presence of another therapist. b) Hard intrusion occurs with a clear explanation to all clients present of its purpose, intent and the desired outcome. c) Hard intrusion is only agreed upon when the client has demonstrated an ability to engage in deep work, and cathect Adult soon after. d) This procedure is done only with the client who is able to cathect Adult, and whose boundaries are defined enough so that the client can take responsibilty for the procedure, before and after it is completed.

Recommended processes: a) Some forms of soft intrusion may be engaged in individual sessions at the therapist's discretion. b) Hard intrusion should only be carried out in a group setting with the agreement of the client, the group and the other therapist. c)Clients with histories of incest, physical abuse, ritual abuse, borderline, histrionic or thought disorders, special sensitivity to establishing a clear contract before proceeding is necessary. d) The client is informed that there may be minor and occasional muscle aching afterwards, because the exercise is often strenuous. A clear boundary between the therapist may be suggested by the use of a folded blanket or pillow between the therapist and the client undergoing the hard intrusion. e) the therapist needs to be in good physical shape.

BIOENERGETIC/PHYSICAL RELEASING PROCEDURES:

Definition: These procedures are aimed at releasing or removing the emotional and physical blockages which are related to archaic emotional trauma and bodyscripting . (Reich, 1970), (Lowen:1970), (Cassius: 1975) (Gowell: 1979). The goal of bioenergetic work is to release stored-up emotions, and to unlock the physical armoring by the client.

Minimum conditions: a)The therapist has had training and experience with the procedures and processes of Bioenergetic therapies (Lowen 19 70). b) The 1-2-3 -STOP rule is clearly understood and used. Both the client and the group understand that by calling 1-2-3 STOP the process is aborted, since "STOP" could be a part of their catharsis.(Experiencing Enough Staff 1985). c) The client contracts with the Adult Ego State to do this work and agrees to be in charge of and later report their inner experience of the process. d) The client needs to have a good understanding of the Passivity (Schiff:1971;Mellor 1975a &b) material and the Self Care Agreements. e)Physical safety is provided for i.e. Mats, pillows, no hard objects within range of the client, enough group members to provide appropriate protection and restraint. f) Bioenergetic theory as developed by Lowen and Reich (1972, 1980) is the basic framework used here. The therapists should be familiar with this material. g) The therapist will stay grounded, will hold the group energy, and will call 1-2-3-STOP when doing so will promote the safety of the client(s).

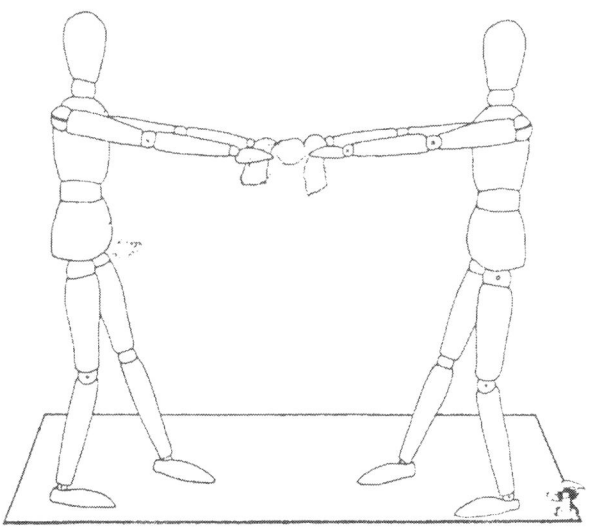

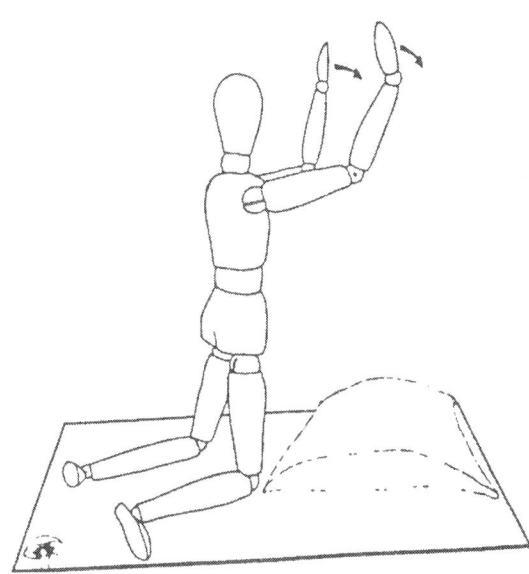

Recommended processes: a)Removal of watches, jewelry, eyeglasses, contacts, belt buckles, hair clips by all participants. b) Restraints (rage or fear) - procedure in which the client is held on the mat in a specific manner so that safety and protection are provided so that the client can go "out of control" and drop into an altered state of consciousness. (Perls "lose your mind and come to your senses"). 1. Five to seven individuals are needed to restrain the client - One on each arm (two), One on each thigh (two) One at the head, one on lower legs, one on wrists (two). 2.A towel is available at the head for use if the forehead becomes sweaty, or if the client wishes to bite on it. 3.Never restrain over the joints, to allow some movement. 4. Pay attention to the client's breathing -stop if client holds breath, lips turn blue or if the skin becomes pasty, or if client is unable to release the energy. 5. check-in frequently with the client to be sure that the process is appropriate. 6. Encourage the client to use sound and breath as a release. 7.Another option for a restraint is to wrap the client in a sheet, shoulders to feet with arms at side. In the case of the sheet restraint 3-4 individuals are needed to restrain the client: one at head, one on each arm(two) , one over the legs 8.Racket or bat hitting on a pillow - procedure providing safety when the client needs to hit. Breathing and sound are attended to. The client uses both hands on the racket/bat/rubber hose and swings it straight over the head, using the whole body. Others and property are kept out of range of the swing. 9.Tantrum - procedure in which the client may lie down on the mat and safely release energy without restriction of a restraint. Provide protection for heels and for hands (pillows, mat, futon). Spotters are assigned at hard surface areas to keep client from hitting the floor. 10. Towel Pull - procedure providing safety when the client needs to express feelings through pulling on a towel. No letting go of the towel until after the 1-2-3-STOP is called. No jerking of the towel - use a steady pull. Spotters at hard surface areas - door knobs, walls, desks etc. It is recommended that the client be grounded (bioenergetic procedure) before and after these procedures. This process allows the client to learn on a somatic level how to release and contain energy more evenly and to connect with their own inner nurturing and strength. 11. Often being held in a nurturing posture after intense release is another source of grounding and offers support for the further release of feelings. It is also useful for the client to ground after being held. Clients who have engaged in energy work are often in an altered state of consciousness and must be checked out for a functioning Adult before leaving group.

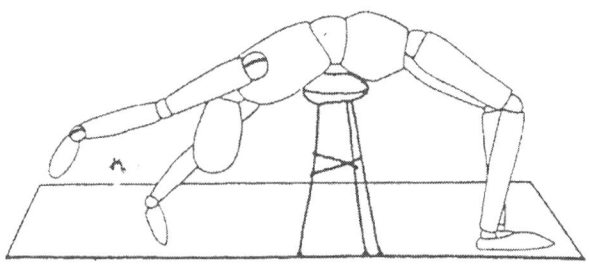

BREATH WORK:

Definition: Breath work (Reich: 1970) (Lowen :1958) and (Grof: 1993) uses hyperventilation and breathing energetic techniques to distract the conscious mind and allow unconscious memories or feelings to emerge. It is one of the methods for moving the individual from ordinary to non-ordinary reality, and back. It provides a good experience of an altered state of consciousness in which archaic material may be released to consciousness.

Minimum conditions: a) the therapist has been trained in the process of breath work. b) The environment is safe - pillows are available to protect the client's body; all hard objects are removed, and if the therapy room is not sound-proofed neighbors are informed to expect the loud noises so that the police are not summoned. c) The client is able to cathect Adult to institute the process, and to end the process. d) The client is physically healthy. e) The client has a clear understanding of the process and its purposes. f) There is sufficient time to carry out the process and return the client to Adult functioning, and normal consciousness. g) The client is in therapy or is a therapy graduate with access to therapy for any needed follow-up work or additional processing. h) The client must have fully returned to ordinary reality i.e. normal waking consciousness before leaving the location of the Breath Work.

SHOCK AND TRAUMA RESPONSES:

This is a very important factor when dealing with any kind of psychotherapy, especially body work. The client and the Therapists need to be aware of the way in which a person goes into SHOCK. This is highly idiosyncratic and each person will have their own perceptual triggers. This condition arises when a person's autonomic nervous system goes automatically into either parasympathetic shock or sympathetic shock When this happens all systems shut down and the person is unable to use their cerebral function, to THINK. They move immediately into FIGHT, FLIGHT OR FREEZE. Freeze is the parasympathetic shock and has its roots deeply in prenatal and perinatal experience. It will usually manifest with pallor and shallow breathing. Fight and flight are sympathetic responses to trauma which occurred a little later in pre and perinatal experiences. The person in parasympathetic shock will get red, breathless, and sometimes very pale. Most individuals are able to recognize the precursors of their shock response and noting this can devise a system to allow them to recover their cerebral functions sufficiently to set up a process to solve the problem. It is important for the therapist and the client to begin early in therapy with the recognition of this response and with the setting up of the individual's ability to deal with it appropriately.

> In the dark time
> Will there be singing?
> Yes, there will also be singing
> About the dark times.
> Berthold Brecht

LEAVING THE GROUP:

Definition: when a client terminates or suspends (takes a leave of absence) from therapy group.

Minimum conditions: a) there should be an identified process for leaving group agreed to, by the client and therapist, before the client enters group. b) this process will allow for some orderly way of reviewing the client's reasons for leaving and providing feedback (this procedure usually takes 3-4 sessions). c) if the client is to be charged for missing the checkout processing session(s) (ie runs from group) this must be agreed upon in writing before the beginning of therapy and signed by the client.

Recommended procedure for leaving group: This is a three week process. First week: The client indicates their intention to leave group and receives feedback, and hears the other group members' reactions . Second Week: Client reviews their contracts and accomplishments and receives feedback, and congratulations on these. Third week: Group members "celebrate" with a ritual the leaving and thus achieve closure on the client's exit. This allows persons with abandonment issues to acknowledge and deal with them and the leaving does not come as a sudden and unexpected event.

RUNNING/PHYSICAL ESCALATION:

Definition: This is a situation in which a client becomes excessively scared or angry and either starts to leave the group setting without appropriate support, and may be potentially or actually verbally or physically violent, or does not return to therapy giving little or no notice of their decision, i.e. they leave in a regressed state.

Minimum conditions: The therapist will confront the escalation by using the agreed upon "stop all activity" statement (such as 1-2-3-STOP). Groups will always have such statements in their language.

Recommended conditions: a) the therapist(s) and group may physically block the client from running (i.e. stand in front of the door). The therapist will encourage the client to THINK about what is happening, to invite Adult activity. If the client persists in leaving, the therapist will not hinder the client from doing so. b) In the case of suicidal or homicidal tendencies the therapist may utilize physical restraint to protect the escalated client and others from the violent behavior. The therapist will not endanger self or the clients. c) the police or the mental health professionals will be notified if this is appropriate. d) the therapist will stay aware of the effect of the escalation on the other group members and invite discussion of thoughts, feelings etc. about the escalation. e) follow up of the escalation with the client and the group is recommended.

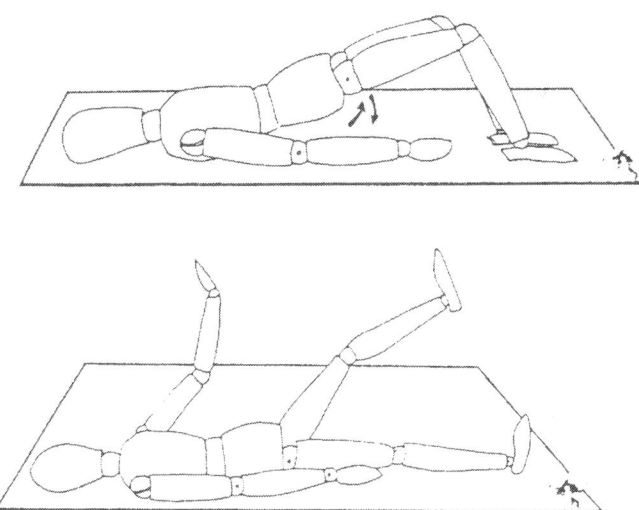

Temper tantrums and pelvic pounding are structured as supported escalation.

ABSENCE OF THE THERAPIST:

Definition: When the primary therapist(s) are going to be absent from regularly scheduled group sessions.

Minimum conditions: a) A backup therapist will be provided if both therapists are to be absent; b) when possible, the time the therapist will be absent will be announced at least three weeks in advance; c) if no backup therapist can be provided then the group session will either be cancelled or rescheduled to a date when a therapist can be provided. In the event the group wishes to meet in the absence of a therapist, they are advised that this constitutes an "unofficial group" and there are no charges for the meeting. They may meet at one of the group members house d) It is made clear that attendance at any group, except for the therapists, is voluntary.

CLEARINGS AND CHECKING OUT FANTASIES:

Definition : When the client makes statements and asks questions in order to validate, clear up, or change his or her understanding of an event or an exchange with others.

Minimum conditions: This process is given highest priority to allow clients to be fully present in ordinary reality so that they will feel safe to do highly charged emotional work. a) In clearings, people have an opportunity to check out projections, explore beliefs about self and others, and ask for what they need and want. b)The language used excludes blaming, judging i.e. no Drama Triangle (Karpman: 1968). c) they may not ask for changes in behavior, simply to be heard. d) The person who is being cleared with is first asked if they are willing to hear the clearing. e) The process is carefully tracked by the therapist and group in order to intervene if the person who is clearing becomes confused or persecutory. The recommended process is as follows:

The Clearing Structure:

I felt _____(mad, sad, scared or glad)
because when you_____(describe the behavior, in detail without embellishment)
I think it means about me_____(my script belief),
What I need from you is_____(e.g. to be heard).
What I need for myself is_____(e.g. to say this).

The process is often completed with the person checking a fantasy: e.g. "My fantasy is that you think I am bad, is that true?" (Garcia:1982).

Everyone takes the limits of his own
vision for the limits of the world.
Arthur Schopenhauer

ASSISTANTS: (intern, "older sibling" etc):

Definition: An assistant is a professional e.g. in graduate education in counseling, three or more years of Corrective Parenting therapy other psychotherapeutic education or training, and at least six months of personal Corrective Parenting therapy group experience. This is a person seeking further training, or a graduate of a Corrective Parenting group who desires the experience of being an intern, assistant or "older sibling", and wishing to support the group process. Role: To be in training, learning more about the process of corrective parenting and their own process, as well as, to help the therapist with the clients' process. An assistant or intern may not take the role, even for one group, of the primary therapist unless they are licensed or certified or registered in their state.

Minimum conditions: a) There is a clear agreement between each assistant/intern and primary therapist of the assistant/intern role. b) Clear understanding of reciprocity in the agreement that the trainee receives training and the therapist receives the benefit of a "helper" in the group. c)Assistants/interns adopt the Code of Ethics Corrective Parenting d) The Primary therapist is responsible for supervising assistants during group and for assessing their ability to maintain appropriate boundaries during work. e) Assistants/interns will have regular staffing and feedback sessions with primary therapist. f) The ethical standards apply to assistants in all situations.

And now here is my secret, a very
Simple secret: it is only with the
heart that one can see rightly;
what is essential is invisible to the eye.
St. Exupery

Elaine Childs Gowell, PhD and Sharon Glantz

CONCLUSION:

In the process of providing treatment for persons whose life experience has been profoundly traumatizing and deeply scarring, it is necessary to use some approaches to their issues which address the neurobiological, ontogenetic and developmental aspects of their pathology. In some instances extraordinary approaches are needed to effect the changes these persons are seeking, and deserve. Since much of their trauma has occurred at a preverbal time in their lives, and directly affects the limbic system and the midbrain and amygdala, no amount of talking will bring these experiences into consciousness, nor will it be possible to heal these experiences with talking methods. It is absurd to assume that we can access the limbic brain or even the more primitive neo-cortex with language which is cerebral and more advanced developmentally. Knowing this, Rituals (procedures) have been devised to reach the client's trauma at the neurological level at which it is seated. Because these Rituals (procedures) often require the individual to reach an altered state of consciousness (ASC) which addresses the neurological base of the disorder, movement, touch, activity, are undertaken to reach the pathology where it is seated. Since these Rituals and processes are extraordinary, and in some cases, invasive, there must be some rules established so that the client and practitioner engage in them in ways which are protective of both the client and the therapist. The power differential in Positive Transference Therapies must be addressed and the position of the client protected . So often the unconscious delegation of power is to the therapist from the client. Therefore, the Standards of Practice which make up this publication have been established to provide such protection, and clarification of position on the OKAY CORRAL (Ernst:1974) The goal of therapy is to empower the client, and in order for the client and therapist to have permission to cross the "dangerous bridge" between ordinary and non ordinary reality, these rules have been put forward. The provision of psychic opening and heightened awareness and receptivity to learning comes through the pathway of Ritual process (procedures and techniques). The process must be structured in such a way as to encourage the expression of the underlying neurological experience of the participant. Where these processes may be in contravention of the established regulations of the professional and state organizations, the practitioner needs to have a safe and scientifically based structure by which to carry out the processes. These Standards of Practice for Corrective Parenting Regression, and Rechilding are an attempt to set structures for the safety and the effectiveness of the Rituals and processes defined above. The philosophical position "without structure, there is no freedom" is thus carried out. Forces in the unconscious when channeled into Psychotherapy Rituals can, and do create a transformational experience for the client and the group. "When shared, they result in synergy instead of entropy," (Childs-Gowell: 1979: p 225) for the client and the group and a release of energy on the psychic level resulting in healing and health.

Love has earth to which she clings. Robert Frost

PART II:

CONTRACTING FOR REGRESSIVE WORK: CORRECTIVE PARENTING AND RECHILDING: THE SELF CARE CONTRACTS: ACCOUNTABILITY WORK (THE "CORNER")

Closing "escape hatches" or "loop holes" and
the work which arises from the therapeutic
activity of confronting and examining the
breaking of these agreements.

ELAINE CHILDS GOWELL
MN. MPH. ARNP. PhD. C.T.A.

Full time private practice as a Psychosocial Nurse and
Clinical Anthropologist

SUMMARY: PART II:

This section describes the "Healing Rituals" known as the Self Care Contracts. These contracts serve to close the escape hatches (Holloway (1973), Boyd and Boyd(1980) which people use to further their script behaviors. The article defines Escape Hatches, and Self Care Contracts and describes how the process of Accountability Work (also known as The Corner, The Think Chair, or Time Out). For people whose socialization was inadequate or meager. The process assists clients to think about feelings, feel about thoughts and order their thought processes. It is an empowering intervention for thought disordered, and other clients, and much appreciated by those who engage in it.

CONTRACTING FOR REGRESSIVE WORK:

CORRECTIVE PARENTING AND RECHILDING: THE SELF CARE CONTRACTS: ACCOUNTABILITY WORK AKA "COR-NER".

INTRODUCTION:

An article by Brook (1996) with regard to Permission, reminded the present author that the use of Self Care Contracts is a form of Permission. One of the regressive therapies developed from reparenting, over the past twenty years is a therapeutic process known as corrective parenting. Permission and safety are provided in corrective parenting through a number of processes which known as "Healing Rituals" (van de Hart 1978). A "Healing Ritual" is a process in which clients may re-experience archaic and traumatic events, and change the experience from the old system (trauma) to the new system (healing). These Rituals provide the clients with a structure within which they can grow away from their old script behaviors. Many of these rituals provide the permission needed to break scripts, and become "warriors of the heart". Among the very important processes, or if you will, "healing rituals" are the Self Care Contracts. Many of the people who come for therapy have defined themselves as Adult Children of Dysfunctional Parents. Many of them lack the socialization skills which accrue to persons growing up in healthier families. Most clients in psychotherapy are suffering profound grief for the mistreatment they had as children. The Good Grief Rituals described by Childs-Gowell (1992) are examples of "Healing, Rituals" which can be self-administered by the reader. Another resource for healthy parenting are Weiss and Weiss (1988), Weinhold and Weinhold (1992) and James(1981). Among the

Rituals which work better in a group setting, and offered to our clients are the Self Care Contracts. When personally, when the author was participating in this process for personal growth, needing to heal a frightened and traumatized child who governed adult life, the self care contracts were invaluable. Some of the traumas this author experienced were at the level of deep shock. As an adult child of a battering mother, and a fearful, and passive father, there was a deep need for a therapist who would offer a strong "healthy parent" from which to model and incorporate a personal healthy parent. This healthy parent had to have the power to protect the frightened child and also be powerful enough to give permission (Crossman:1966) to go into the terror and horror, and to find the healing resources inside the self. The healthy parent selected had to be more powerful than the archaic crazy and abusive parent. The therapist who would model a new healthy parent had to be able to provide protection from the internal abusive parent. Needed was someone who could 'take care' of the archaic parent's crazy child parts (the child within the archaic parent, within), and would give permission to LIVE, to BE, to DO, to THINK, and to FEEL and to be real , to be empowered to succeed in life from a personal and spiritual depth, rather than from script. This permission had to be powerful enough so that all the old unfinished, and painful pieces of archaic business that were still blocking life, could be explored. The therapy offered the oppportunity to live life as fully as one's birth right demands, fulfilling de Chardin's (1965) invitation to Be "a spiritual being on a human path", not be a human being searching for spirit somewhere. The need to become fully bonded with SELF loving SELF unconditionally, and interdependent with others is very powerful. This therapy offered an opportunity to let go of being filled with self-hatred, to let go of the constant fear of making a full commitment to life and to others. This bonding is probably the most important part of Being a human being, and yet so many parents do not, and did not understand that "giving their children everything" was no substitute for the deep spiritual bond that all human babies and adults seek. Many clients who lack this bonding and attachment have to attach and bond with their therapist at a deep "baby" level before they can truely examine and correct what "went wrong". From the bonded place, a client is then able to bond with self and come to love and cherish their own "baby self". There is considerable evidence from practice that the "baby self" is the part of us who is closest to the spiritual self. The bonding process takes clients through the steps of checking out whether this therapist is 'competent' to model a healthy parent for their child. For some people this checking-out and trusting process takes a fairly long time, and they sometimes have to go through several therapists before the "right" one is found. Some clients never complete the healthy positive transference that they need to be able to successfully carry through with their therapeutic experience, to go the whole distance, all the way to total health and happiness. Perhaps one of the reasons some therapists cannot offer total healing is because they themselves have not gone the distance. It is understood that it is difficult for some therapists to accept the self-care contracts as prescriptions, and some clients "feel contained" (Mothersole 1996) by the agreements. Nevertheless the experience among the corrective parenting community therapists has been that there are some who need and welcome this "containment" as a safety measure. Even the rebellious ones will admit that it "saved their life" to be offered such containment. The choice of therapists is often unerring, and many are fortunate to have the 'right' therapist for each part of their process. Finally when it becomes imperative for the client to face their very deepest fears, the deepest somatic traumas, their "baby needs", if they are fortunate, they find a therapist who was able to say to them in essence: " I will be a Healthy Parent for your baby. I will take care of your baby under contract, until you can do it yourself." Also " I can handle your archaic parent's crazy child so that you can be free to be a healthy child yourself, and so you can experience a healthy childhood". In essence what is said to them is: "it's never too late to have a happy childhood".(Landsman: 1984). The structure provided by the self care contracts empowers them to proceed in challenging their old script, and provides the therapeutic process with added protection and empowerment.

THE LIFE SCRIPT INTERVIEW:

In general the practice of the process of corrective parenting therapy starts with a general Life Script Interview as exemplified by Holloway (1975),Levin's (1982) Developmental Life Script Questionnaire, and the format for eliciting this information taught by Muriel James (1980) . These are powerful tools which permit the therapist to elicit important information for their client's process. These questionnaires and interviews have assisted many therapists in their own process. The ability to to acknowledge that our families were truly dysfunctional in ways that have impacted us adversely is empowering, and a vital first step. In the beginning of treatment the clients are asked to take responsibility for the changes they need to make their own lives better. An exploration is undertaken of the steps that are necessary to be able to meet personal life goals, fulfill the life vision, and actualize self fully. These tools help the therapist, and are invaluable to clients, to get past denial, and the mistaken beliefs that their family was "healthy". As therapists we have clients review their life goals, and what their expectations are of the therapist. These are couched in the language of long-term and short-term contracts. The contracts are underwritten theoretically by the therapeutic intervention known as "closing escape hatches" (Holloway:1974; Boyd and Boyd:1979;

and Boyd: 1986). This process offers a profound level of protection from their "escape hatches". These "outs" are devised by the desperate and despairing child at stages when the world is not clear to them. It is not unusual for abused and battered children to vow that if "things get bad enough, I can always ......run away, kill myself, get sick etc. and then they'll be sorry they ever abused me." These vows, also known as "decisions" (Goulding:1979), become a part of the unconscious motivation for facing life as a grown-up. Probably one of the most important structures of permission to come out of the early Transactional Analysis theory is the development of the self care contracts.

THE SELF CARE CONTRACTS:

These contracts are couched in negative language ie "I do not.." because they speak to the part of the person who made the early decision, the vow. i.e. the defense/survival system. ("I will not" implies in the future, and "I won't" implies Child). These contracts make it clear that this form of therapy is serious, and safe, and that the therapist really cares, and is truly powerful (ie more powerful than the crazy parts of one's parent within). Over the years, clients have claimed these contracts to be the most powerful tool for guiding them to achieve their goals in life. In many ways the contracts provide the same level of empowerment that the Twelve Steps do. These contracts address the underlying issues in the personality structure. When clients have difficulty keeping any one of these contracts, they become aware of what the script issues i.e. "mistaken beliefs" are which are generating the contract-breaking i.e. self sabotaging behaviors, and which need to be worked on and cleared up. Often the "mistaken belief" is couched in the language of :"lies we tell ourselves". When a contract is broken, "time out" or thinking time is set aside so that the client can figure out what the therapeutic issues are and which regression technique or therapeutic intervention is needed in order to make the necessary script changes on a deeper psychological or somatic level. The client, group, and therapist collaborate in devising the most effective intervention needed. In some therapeutic communities this time out is known as the "corner" where the individual takes time to think about the issues involved in breaking the contract. More recently because of the connotation of the "corner " being punitive, this time out is called "the think chair" or as in the Medicine Wheel teachings, "going to the West", or "Accountability Work". The West being the direction in which one faces issues of personal integrity on the Medicine Wheel. (Villoldo: 1988). The self care contracts are as follows:

I DO NOT KILL MYSELF ACCIDENTLY OR ON PURPOSE, NOR DO I CONTRIBUTE TO MY DYING.(Boyd:1986). This contract addresses the existential issues which many clients face. It has become evident in practice and in the personal process of the therapists who use it, and in that of many of the clients, that if there are pre-conception, (Emerson 1992), pre-and-perinatal, or very early childhood issues underlying, the managment of this contract can become deeply challenging. This contract was very important to the author, because through it we discovered that there was a very young part of the personality that was in rage at the mother for not lactating at birth, for not feeding the baby and then for turning it over to a wet nurse. We discovered that despair is often very deep over these issues and contributes to the client's failure to be fully committed to this life. The author succeeded in life, using the rage at the abandoning mother from which to succeed, rather than succeeding from a deep spiritual committment to life. This seems also to be true for many clients. In confronting and dealing with the behaviors around breaking this contract it is possible to uncover the decisions made that were impeding a full commitment to life. I DO NOT HARM MYSELF OR OTHERS, NOR DO I PROVOKE OTHERS TO HARM ME. I STAY SAFE, I RESPECT OTHERS AND MYSELF AND ACT IN A RESPONSIBLE MANNER. Through this contract, clients have succeeded in facing up to a number of harmful habits they have developed. Included among these are habits many clients come into therapy for: obsessive compulsive and co-dependent behaviors which make up many life scripts. Obviously, those whose families were abusive will find that not harming self or others is a large challenge, and breaking this agreement often directs them to a great deal of their therapeutic process. I DO NOT GET SICK OR GO CRAZY. I STAY SANE AND HEALTHY AND WORK THROUGH MY PROBLEMS RESPONSIBLY BY STRUCTURING MY WORK WITHIN A THERAPEUTIC CONTRACT. As children, and later as adults, many clients do not have permission to express their feelings freely or appropriately. The author's own experience was with an explosive mother. This behavior, of storing up feelings until they cannot be contained anymore, and ending in an escalation is a common experience for many clients. This is not a healthy adult form of functioning. It is true for many people in this culture, that they do not believe that they can get their needs met in healthy ways, and they use sickness and crazy acting-out behaviors, in unsucessful attempts to get some of their needs met. This contract creates a climate in which the client can start facing some of the issues around getting needs met appropriately. Clients find it very helpful in learning how not to escalate around getting needs met, and how to take care of themselves so that they are able to express their thoughts and feelings appropriately. The interventions constructed around the breaking of this contract are numerous and deeply healing. Imagine having to deal with the ways in which one gets sick, colds, the flu, headaches, and not take a cavalier attitude, but actually look at what script may be operating when one does get sick? It is a fact of this society that the only time many of us could get nurturing from a parent was when we were sick, and then the parent was very good to us. Getting sick is for many of us, one way to get nurture, and positive strokes.

I DO NOT RUN AWAY PHYSICALLY OR PSYCHOLOGICALLY; I STAY, WORK THROUGH MY FEELINGS, THOUGHTS, AND BEHAVIORS AND SOLVE PROBLEMS. This contract is very important to many as it helps to focus on the ways in which they avoid doing what is needed to be done in the therapeutic process. Clients find that the habits of script are so strong that it is easy to side step, run from, or slip by some important issues. Those whose lifestyle is that of the 'workaholic', recognize how they use working hard to run away from issues. Running away serves many people well in modern urban society, and until the clients start living by the self-care contracts, it seems normal behavior to run or engage in running behaviors. As a child, running away is very effective in an abusive environment because one can avoid many a beating or tongue lashing. When the child returns to the household, the parent may have forgotten their rage, and they once more escaped another punishing thrashing. This behavior also interferes with intimacy. This contract helps clients to become aware of all of the slick and sneaky ways they have of running away. Learning about running behaviors helps to raise consciousness about life style, life programming as sneaky behaviors. I AM NOT SNEAKY, AND I DO NOT LIE. I DO NOT STEAL. I AM HONEST WITH MYSELF AND OTHERS BOTH INTELLECTUALLY AND EMOTIONALLY. This contract means that the client will be honest about their thoughts and feelings, and not sneak or fudge or twist the truth in order to get by as so many of us had to do in our families of origin. This contract is of importance to most of us in that we have to recognize the ways in which we are out of integrity with self, family, and associates. The client comes to realize how defensive they have become to cover their feelings of scare about being "found out". This is often the last contract for a client in ongoing treatment to address. It is often a benchmark that the individual is finally individuated, and able to behave in ways which are not symbiotic, or co-dependent, and they are able to recognize deal with all of the ways in which they are being and have been sneaky in their lives. I AM NOT PASSIVE, I AM PROACTIVE TO MY OWN AND OTHERS' THOUGHTS, FEELINGS AND BEHAVIORS. The passive behaviors are outlined by the various people who wrote about them in the 1970's (Schiff et al 1972; Mellor:1976). As outlined in these writings, passivity and the discounting engaged in to remain passive is described as four behaviors which invite symbiosis. These behaviors are in increasing amount of energy needed to carry each one out: do nothing; overadapt; agitate; and escalate (either implosively or explosively). Passive behavior is learned very young, probably in the womb and thereafter. It is difficult to overcome without careful attention to archaic issues. Attending to passivity and discounting is a very dynamic guide to cognitive restructuring. Paying attention to these behaviors helps the client deal with what is going on in the moment. It makes it difficult to redefine, to remain silent, to ignore, minimize or maximize whatever may be going on in the present. Attention to passive behaviors reinforces personal accountability. It is the basic contract for everything one does in a healthy and accountable adult life. Passive behaviors are seen to be the dynamic which underlies everything we do that may be codependent or symbiotic. Passive behaviors are found to underlie all of the above contracts, since one has to engage in passivity to utilize any one of the escape hatches. In the author's and clients' process it is frequently evident how fortunate we were to have been guided through this process by healthy therapists and teachers in Transactional Analysis. In the Seattle community there are a number of therapists who have personally benefited from this process, having themselves experienced the Rituals involved in Corrective Parenting and Rechilding. The Healing Rituals arising from the close attention to the passive behaviors in ourselves and our clients have aided many people to free themselves from their scripts.

ACCOUNTABILITY WORK:

THE CORNER: WEST WORK: THE THINK CHAIR: These are terms used to cover the process of confronting the breaking of a self-care contract. In this process the client usually self confronts and takes "time out" to THINK ABOUT the how, why and underlying issues in the breaking of a self care contract. It also is followed when a peer or a therapist confronts the breaking of a self care contract. The client is expected to accept the confrontaton and do their "thinking" without defending or rationalizing. (BDDREJJ = Blame. Defend. Doubt. Rationalize. Explain. Justify. Judge.) The clients are given a structure for doing this because often the issue is generated in script, and is often in the client's "blind spot". The process which is recommended is as follows:

The contract I broke is _____(one of the self care contracts, or a contract they have attached to accountability work). How I broke it is_____(outline the manner in which it was broken). The Mistaken Belief or Script issue underlying the breaking of the contract is_____The Adult work I will do to challenge this Mistaken Belief (Core or Limiting Belief) (Cognitive Restructuring work, affirmation exercises etc.) The Child work I will do is _____ (Regressive work which addresses the developmental stage or the early decision and challenges it). What I learned from breaking this contract is_____. Clients find this ritual/process very empowering in learning to cathect Adult, and take charge of their own therapy. It is a very powerful tool for the therapists, particularly if they themselves are actively engaged in confronting these same issues.

CONCLUSION:

These Healing Rituals are offered by paying close attention to the "Self Care Contracts" and to the processes revolving around breaking contracts. Checking out one's thinking and coming clear about the underlying issues have been found to be very dynamic in helping a client discover core isses where they need to do their healing work. In finding ways to challenge the "mistaken beliefs" underwriting so much of the breaking of the contracts, they find that they are in charge of their own healing process. Clients who learn more and more about their own psychological structure, have more and more psychic openings, and increasing freedom from Script. Those clients who release themselves from their Script, are able to take more responsibility for their lives. This process itself, is an empowering experience, because as one engages in the process of agreeing to and breaking contracts, of recommitting to SELF and to the Self Care Contracts constitutes an opportunity for individuals to gain social skills which are useful in family and workplace. The Self Care Contracts make it possible for people to parent themselves in healthier ways, thus creating better parents out there in the world for the little ones who are coming along behind them. The use of the Self Care Contracts is a profoundly political and spiritual intervention for "Adult children" of any negative history. This process works in profound ways, and has healed many clients who have undertaken the "Warrior-of-the Heart" Path.

> What locks itself in endurance grows rigid;
> sheltered in unassuming grayness, does it
> feel safe? Wait, from the distance hardness
> is menaced by something still harder. Alas -:
> a remote hammer is poised to strike.
> Rainer Maria Rilke

REFERENCES:

Adler, A. (1932). The Practice and Theory of Individual Psychology New York. Harcourt Brace and Company

Berne, E. (1961) Transactional Analysis in Psychotherapy: A systematic individual and social psychiatry. New York. Grove Press.

Berne, E. (1964) Games People Play. New York. Grove Press

Boyd, H.S., & Cowles-Boyd, L. (1980). Blocking Tragic Scripts. Transactional Analysis Journal, 10,227-229.

Cassius, J. (1980) Bodyscripts. Mimeograph copy.

Childs-Gowell, E. (1979) Reparenting Schizophrenics: the Cathexis Experience. North Quincy, Massachusetts. The Christopher House.

Childs-Gowell, E. (1978). Bodyscript Blockbusting. Seattle. Wa. (self published)

Childs-Gowell E. (1988) Stages of Ages: A handbook of Corrective Parenting.Seattle. Wa. (self published)

Childs-Gowell, E. (1992) Good Grief Rituals. New York. Station Hill Press.

de Chardin, T. (1965) The Phenomenon of Man. New York. Harper. Torchbooks.

Clarke, J.I .and Dawson C. (1989) Growing Up Again. San Francisco. Ca. Harper and Row.

Eliade, M. (1969). The Quest: History and Meaning in Religion. Chicago . University of Chicago Press.

Erickson, M. (1980).The Collected Papers of Milton H. Erickson on Hypnosis ` (E.L. Rossi, Ed) New York. Irvington Publishers.

Emerson, W. 1987-1994: Pre and Perinatal workshops. Seattle, Petaluma, and San Francisco. Ca

Garcia. P. Reactivity. Transactional Analysis Journal. Vol 12.2 pp 123-126

Grof, S. (1985) Beyond the brain : Birth Death and Transcendence in Psychotherapy. Albany, New York. State University of New York. Press.

Grof, S. with Bennet H. (1990) The Holotropic Mind. San Francisco. Harper-Collins.

Grof, S. (1998)The Cosmic Game. New York. State University of New York.

Goulding, M & Goulding, R. (1979) Changing Lives Through Redicision Therapy. New York. Bruner/ Mazel

Holloway, W. (1973) Shut the Escape Hatch. Monograph series (pp15-118) Medina , Oh: Midwest Institute for Human Understanding.

James, M. (1981) Breaking Free: Breaking Free for a New Life. Reading. Ma. Addison Wesley.

Karpman, S. (1968) Fairy Tales and Script Drama Analysis. Transactional Analysis Bulletin VII 26:33- 43

Landsman , S. (1984) Found a Place for Me. Treehouse EnterprIses . Farmington Hills. Mi

Levin, P. (1988) Cycles of Power: A user's guide to the seven seasons of life. Deerfield Beach, Fl. Health Communications.

Lowen, A. (1980) Bioenergetics. New York. Lancer Books

Lucas, W. (1995) Regression Therapy; a Handbook for Professionals: Volumes I & II . Illinois. Deep Forest Press.

Marcher, E. (1996). Personal communication . San Francisco. CA.

Mellor, K. Passivity. Transactional Analysis Journal. V (pp295-302)

Mellor, K. Redefining. Transactional Analysis Journal V. (303-311)

Moreno, J (1959) Psychodrama in Arieti: Handbook of Psychiatry II. New York. 1375-1376.

Peplau, H. (1964) Workshop on psychiatry for nurses, lectures and Clinical experiences based on Harry Stack Sullivan. Chicago. Il.

Perls. F (1969) Gestalt Therapy Verbatim. New York. Bantam

Reich, W. (1972) Character Analysis. New York. Simon and Schuster

Schaeffer, B. (1984) Corrective Parenting Chart. Wisconsin

Schiff. J et al (1075 The Cathexis Reader. New York. Harper and Row

Schiff,J. and Schiff, A. (1971) Passivity. Transactional Analysis Journal (1) pp71-78

Steiner, C. (1971) The Stroke Economy. Transactional Analysis Journal (3) pp9-15

Sullivan, H.S. (1958) The Interpersonal Theory of Psychiatry. New York, WW. Norton

Van der Hart, O. (1978) Rituals in Psychotherapy. New York. Irvington Pubs.

PART III

BUDDHA'S "MIDDLE WAY" and CORRECTIVE PARENTING'S "MIDDLE GROUND: A COMPARISON OF THE STRUCTURE AND THE ALTERED STATES OF CONSCIOUSNESS OF TRANSACTIONAL ANALYSIS' CORRECTIVE PARENTING AND THE TEACHINGS OF THE ANCIENT SPIRITUAL PATH OF BUDDHISM

by ELAINE CHILDS GOWELL PHD

FROM CHAOS TO ORDER:

The paradigm shift described by Thomas Kuhn,(1962) Marilyn Ferguson, (1973) Fritjof Capra (1996) and others is upon us. We, on this planet seem to be rapidly reaching the point of critical mass when the old paradigm which, I believe, is a fear and violence-based paradigm and the new paradigm which is love and compassion-based meet at a crossroads. At times of paradigm shifts there is always chaos as the old structures no longer work and "everything seems to be falling apart". The theory of Dissipative Structures by Nobel Laureate in Physics Ilya Prigogine (1984) describes this type of event when all the pieces of the old structure dissipate leaving a time of chaos before some of them come back together again in a new and stronger form of organization. In the mental health field we are seeing increasing need for services to deal with the chaos people are experiencing. The emergency rooms and mental health services are being taxed to their maximum. The chaos is being escalated by the conservative reform   movement which is summarily and selfishly cutting funds and services. However, these reform attitudes are all a part of the chaos which is necessary before a new structure is in place.

PRACTITIONER HEAL THYSELF:

More and more mental health practitioners are themselves experiencing a Spiritual crisis as they try to solve the problems with clients who are mirroring their own dysfunction, and longing for spiritual expression. What can they do? As a Shaman/psychotherapist of some 35 years, my clients, colleagues and I have developed a systematic healing model which follows Transactional Analysis (Berne 1961, 1973) and Reparenting (Schiff et al 1975). It is a neurobiologically based process. The process and structure created carries the title of "Corrective Parenting" because it seeks to install in the client a new structure for Self Care and Self Nurturance: i.e. healthy Self Parenting, and Re-Childing (Childs-Gowell 1979, 1988). The end result is a person whose nervous system has calmed down and who is no longer having to deal with archaic and archetypal internal battering. The negative self-talk and self-doubt that are so destructive are reduced, and in many instances, removed. I have discovered that the spiritual yearning that brings people to psychotherapy can begin to be met by the structure and teachings of Corrective Parenting which are parallel to and in many ways similar to Buddha's "Middle Way" teachings. As a non-violent modality, Buddhism does not seem to have the history of violence that most of the other world religions have had; there have been no wars to push the "Middle Way". Transactional Analysis' basic canon is "I'm Okay You're Okay" i.e. WIN / WIN. There is much about Buddha's "Middle Way" that is parallel to and matches the "Middle Ground" philosophy and the Self-Care Contracts of Corrective Parenting.

CORRECTIVE PARENTING:

Corrective Parenting is a therapeutic method based on Transactional Analysis' Reparenting (Schiff 1972) where the client is taught how to find the Middle Ground in life. (Childs-Gowell 1988) 1. Clients are taught Self Care through a system of contracts or agreements, based on archaic decisions made under duress. These decisions are also known in the literature as "escape hatches" or "loopholes" (Holloway, 1973). The Self Care contracts imply in their application that one must have or learn a deep level of self respect - I'm Okay/You're Okay (Harris and Harris, 1969). 2. One gains Integrity and respect for Self as one uses the contracts for intense self-examination, and therefore develops a deeper respect for Self and others. 3. The Developmental Diagnosis is based on metaphors, language, and symptoms, is the basis of the work with the use of Altered States of Consciousness (ASC). 4. Spiritual Midwifery, offers the opening of the way for the client to begin to honor the search for Self, and one's Spiritual nature. These four major aspects of Corrective Parenting have their parallels in the Buddhist Tantric teachings of the "Middle Way" as follows.

PREREQUISITES TO TANTRA: PREREQUISITES TO CORRECTIVE PARENTING:

1. Surrender/ Renunciation, one gives up the obstacles to union with spirit. 2. The dedicated goal of bodhichitta (selfless service), one's life is one's service. 3. The Correct view of Emptiness, according to the Lama Yeshe is "True renunciation" which implies that eventually one no longer relies on sensory pleasure for ultimate happiness. In other words one uses sensory pleasure to raise the Bliss level, but one does not keep trying to find the insubstantial satisfaction from one's addictive behaviors. Lama Yeshe says (p53) that this does not mean giving up pleasures or denying ourselves happiness. It means giving up expectations about these pleasures. It is the obsessive-compulsive attachment to these pleasures that one is called upon to renounce. In Corrective Parenting one is asked to give up addictions one by one and to do the archaic "work" that is powering the need for the addiction. The archaic and archetypal work are accomplished in altered States of Consciousness (ASC) (Tart: 1975) such as regressive work, feeling work, gestalt, psychodrama, body work, hypnosis, NLP, EMDR, TFT and Shamanic techniques such as drumming, rattling, chanting and dancing, which are not used by all therapists. One must surrender oneself to the process

of examining how one breaks the Self Care contracts and how one clings unconsciously to the underlying "lies" and "mistaken core beliefs" which generate the breaking of the contracts. Therefore the attachment to the CORE BELIEF is renounced, and pieces of inner psyche workout are structured to achieve this. This involves ASC and the shifts of energy which ensue, thus making it possible to give up the "mistaken belief" (i.e. the Script). The belief that causes a lot of suffering is: "my needs are not important and I can't get my needs met in healthy ways, so I have to be sneaky to get what I want or need." This is a common "lie" or delusion which underlies many of the addictive behaviors seen in group therapy in Corrective Parenting. As one progresses towards uncovering one's Core Mistaken Beliefs, and the lies (illusions also called MAYA) one tells oneself, one is more able to detach from the dynamic energy that keeps one attached to the obsessive behaviors and the addictions. Renunciation is the first step in both Tantra and in Corrective Parenting. The process in therapy involves identifying the dysfunctional behaviors and making contracts to heal them, and to give them up. That is, owning the need to do something effective about the quitting of the addictive behaviors, is a form of renunciation. The act of "taking refuge" in Buddhism is paralleled in Corrective Parenting by one choosing to commit to the process and to make it work and by taking seriously the processes involved in clearing one's psyche of the archaic and archetypal material lodged there, by way of the Self Care Contracts.

> Fear not what is not real, never was and never will be.
>
> What is real, always was and cannot be destroyed.
>
> Bhagavad Gita

THE BUDDHIST TANTRIC TEACHINGS OF THE MIDDLE WAY:

This overview is taken from the Lama Yeshe (1982, 1987). The Lama suggests that 1. One must develop a deep well of love and wisdom for oneself and for others. One must have compassion for self before one can have compassion for others. Also self-compassion is a path to Self/soul. In Corrective Parenting, respecting and having compassion for self comes out of working the Self Care Contracts, and regressions to free the Child from the past. 2. Heaven is now. There is no Then or There. Having the integrity to use the Now to release the Then, is characteristic of both systems. 3. The basic energy in the process of transformation is the energy of our own desires. The Lama Yeshe points out that : A. Sensory stimulation is the basic motivation for everything human beings do. In Transactional Analysis Berne points out that the Child Ego State is the generator of energy in the personality. B. In Buddhism the wish to be happy is a resource and one must use the energy of one's desires to transform life into something transcendental. "Desire is the fuel." The Transactional Analysis goal is "its' never too late to have a happy childhood." (Yeshe, 1984; Landsman, 1984). According to Tantra one cannot hope to achieve the goal of Universal and complete happiness by systematically making oneself more and more miserable - wearing a hair shirt, so-to-speak. In Corrective Parenting one says that "its never too late to have a happy childhood" (Landsman: 1984) and the work is towards releasing the archaic and archetypal memories which keep one in the straight jacket, the hair shirt of despair to find the insubstantial satisfaction from one's addictive behaviors. Lama Yeshe says (p 53) that this does not mean giving up pleasures or denying ourselves happiness. It means giving up expectations about these pleasures. It is the obsessive-compulsive attachment to these pleasures that one is called upon to renounce. In Corrective Parenting one is asked to give up addictions one by one and do the archaic "work" that is powering the need for the addiction. The archaic and archetypal work are accomplished in Altered States of Consciousness (ASC) (Tart:1975) such as regressive work, feeling work, gestalt, psychodrama, body work, hypnosis, NLP, EMDR, TFT and Shamanic techniques such as drumming, rattling , chanting, and dancing, which are not used by all therapists. One must surrender oneself to the process of examining how one breaks the Self Care contracts and how one clings unconsciously to the underlying "lies" or "mistaken beliefs" which generate the breaking of the contracts. Therefore the attachment to the "mistaken belief" is renounced, and pieces of inner psyche workout are structured. thus making it possible to give up the mistaken belief (i.e. the Script). The belief that causes a lot of suffering is: "my needs are not important and I can't get my needs met in healthy ways, so I have to be sneaky to get what I want or need." This is a common "lie" or delusion which underlies many of the addictive behaviors seen in group therapy in Corrective Parenting. As one progresses in uncovering one's mistaken beliefs, and the lies (illusions also called Maya) one tells oneself, one is more able to detach from the dynamic energy that keeps one attached to the obsessive behaviors and the addictions. Renunciation is the first step in both Tantra and in Corrective Parenting. The process in therapy involves identifying the dysfunctional behaviors and making contracts to heal them, and give them up. That is, owning the need to do something effective about the quitting the addictive behaviors, is a form of renunciation. The act of "taking refuge" in Buddhism is paralleled in Corrective Parenting by one choosing to commit to the process and to make it work and by taking seriously the processes involved in clearing one's psyche of the archaic and archetypal material by way of the Self Care Contracts. This involves ASC and the shift of energy which ensues.

THE OPEN HEART.

The second step in Tantra is opening the heart and dedicating oneself to the process of enlightenment. The parallels are as follows. The act of dedication in Buddha' way is called bodhichitta and the person who is thus dedicated is a bodhisatva The growth and Self Care and self -healing contracts taken up by the client provide an opportunity for the client to make a commitment to purpose. " I am no longer a Victim of my life"."I am daily writing poetry.""I am putting safe tires on my car." " I am flossing my teeth twice a day". While these may not seem lofty enough for a spiritual path, they show surprisingly how the determination to make the desired changes in one's life reverberates throughout the personality system in many other ways. By growing dedicated to one's own healing, one has more positive energy inside to share with others, and to further one's own process. The process of honoring oneself and others follows the acronym B.D.D.R.E.J.J. (Childs-Gowell 1993). When one no longer engages in any of the activities described below: one is better able to have an open and dedicated heart. The acronym is as follows: B: I do not BLAME others, I take responsibility for my life and actions. Blaming keeps one caught in looking outside oneself for the causes of the problem. D: I do not DEFEND - I am responsible for my thoughts and feelings and actions. Defending keeps one separate from true Self. R: I do not RATIONALIZE my Being, my thoughts and actions. I take responsibility for myself. E: I do not EXPLAIN myself, my Existence, or my actions. I'm Okay in the world. J: I do not JUDGE others or myself, I accept that I and others are Okay as is. You and I are ONE. J: I do not JUSTIFY my actions. I am mindful and reflect on my Self Care. D: I do not DOUBT my Spiritual nature. I work towards accepting that I am "a Spiritual Being on a Human Path" (De Chardin, 1963).This period of opening the heart not only involves intense self-examination but also the altered states which go with the properly supported regressive work of Re-Childing and healthy Self-parenting (James 1982). There may often be a period, in accomplishing the successful bonding of oneself to one's own Child, of a series of contracts involving one in taking a parenting contract with the therapist, and involving the therapist in one's healing work as a "healthy parent." This is seen as a parallel to the Guru-yoga initiation in Tantra where the seeker according to Yeshe, "takes in the good qualities of the guru/teacher, and makes them their own." Opening the heart is not easy and with people who carry deep trauma, it is often accompanied by excruciating pain in the chest as the "frozen heart" begins to thaw out. People need the close attachment to their Guru/therapist (healthy parent) at this juncture. It is often a very frightening and painful time for the one who is engaged in this level of commitment. Reaching the Tantric state of "unbearable compassion" requires a complete dedication to compassion for oneself, especially for the archaic self and for one's family especially if it was an abusive family. Forgiveness and gratitude will eventually follow and later emerges complete and selfless devotion to the service of others (bodhichitta).

EMPTINESS.

The third prerequisite step in Tantra as offered by Lama Yeshe is the Correct View of Emptiness which invites us to free ourselves from dual thinking, to realize that our view of reality is deluded and our belief in the self-existence of things is an invalid concept having nothing to do with the actual way in which things exist. Known as illusion or Maya. (Yeshe: p76) The "Middle Way" avoids the extreme views of self-existence and non-existence, eternalism, nihilism, overestimation, underestimation. We project our sense of Ego-self on external and internal phenomena. This creates a superstitious and dualistic system. When we project Ego-self on others or on our environment, we are unable to find Self. When one is able to cultivate an Empty Mind, one becomes aware of an experience of non-duality in which all conflict and confusion ultimately subside. (Yeshe: p79). When one is in a clean, clear state of mind, one is free to pay full attention to what one is doing and then it will be done well. This state of mind is described as the "Being state" in Corrective Parenting. This is when one is able to simply BE in group and in life, not re-stimulated to archaic and archetypal thoughts and memories. (It is when one can Be wholly and completely in the NOW at all times, one has achieved a form of Emptiness. One no longer has a need to "be right." As Pam Levin said, "You can either be right or let go of your script."(1985). Cultivating a natural unaffected state of consciousness provides a broader, freer understanding of our interdependence and of the web-of-life which connects all of us and which provides a clear and aware state of consciousness. This state comes once one has laid the script messages to rest, and one is no longer at the effect of one's family of origin, or one's archaic and archetypal script. Once one is no longer re-stimulated by the past, whether it is in this lifetime, or in "past lifetimes" one can develop a clear and awake state of consciousness. This allows one to be in the state of continuing and all encompassing Bliss so desired by most who are seeking Self/Soul. Through Tantric Practice and Corrective Parenting, the way becomes open for one to have "an expansive, liberated and all encompassing state of consciousness" (Yeshe p 92). In Corrective Parenting a number of techniques and processes are used which are called Healing Rituals to help the client find the "Middle Ground" and to find the much sought after quietness in their minds. These are addressed at each of the developmental stages of life. 1. BEING, i.e. existential and attachment issues (ages preconception to six months old). Being held, cared for in a regressed state (ASC) with affirmation. 2. BEING DOING and DOING BEING, and exploratory and separation issues (ages six months to eighteen months old) Experiencing separating, connecting, exploring, being supported in those activities. 3.Learning THOUGHT processes which encourage clean and clear thinking, (ages eighteen months to three years). "NO" is a complete sentence and sometimes it is negotiable, and sometimes it is not. Game Group. Accountability Work. Regression to age two. 4. One learns skills in PEER relationships and in accepting one's IDENTITY (ages three to six years old) Issues of sexuality, Ego-structure, beginning Autonomy. Healthy Parenting at that age. 5. One comes to hone one's SKILLS for life to where one feels good about oneself, has incorporated the rules of their culture, and has healthy self-esteem. (ages:six to twelve years). One is supported in Self Parenting and creating one's own healthy rules 6. The last stage before adulthood is a RECYCLE stage where each of the above stages are recycled in order (twelve to eighteen years). Have you ever wondered why a thirteen-year-old often acts like a "baby" and a fifteen-year-old is so opposite and negative? Or have you ever wondered why a thirty-six-year-old has such baby needs, and a thirty-eight year old can be so negative and opposite? Each of these stages offer metaphors for finding out, and rooting out our illusions and delusions One finds out that one's beliefs are not what is really truly, or what happened back then, or what is happening now. We have an opportunity to find what is really "Real." The dysfunction in any of these stages is diagnosed through the medium of metaphors and applied kinesiology.

TANTRA

As outlined by Lama Yeshe Tantra suggests that there are five preliminaries to the practice of Tantra of the Highest form which is "Conscious Dying" (p93). These preliminaries are 1. Initiation and empowerment. 2. Keeping commitments of initiation. 3. Purifying self of obstacles. 4. Accumulating a store of positive energy. 5. Guru-yoga - a good model to emulate, appreciate and copy - to inspire us. The Corrective Parenting model offers all five of these preliminaries. 1. It teaches empowerment, for example the Okay Corral, the decontamination of Ego States. 2.Passivity Confrontation: The Self Care contracts which offer a basis for confronting Passive behaviors (Schiff: 1975) and a basis for making a commitment to one's self care, and keeping the contracts. 3. Purifying oneself of BDDEJJ as described above. This protocol assists one in experiencing a mind free of negativity and offers a process for purifying oneself of dysfunctional and negative patterns of thinking. 4. We may start accumulating a store of positive strokes in order to feel good and stop the Games and Rackets (Berne:1973) which one uses to manipulate those around us. All of the TA Gestalt, psychodrama, affirmation exercises, stroke circles, holding, massaging, pons stimulation, and healthy touching offer one a release of positive endorphins to one's system providing a rich resource of positive energy from which one can draw, to enhance the experience of Bliss and an Open Heart. 5.Guru Yoga: This offers inspiration, and one is supported in making a parenting contract which provides one with a constant and ever present in one's thoughts of the modeling of healthy compassion, unconditional loving and full acceptance. Needless to say, the therapists must themselves be models of clarity of consciousness, compassion and unconditional loving and clear Ego States - that is, practice non-dual wisdom. When one has reached the point in Corrective Parenting where one is practiced in both the preliminary steps, where one does not B.D.D.R.E.J.J. Having surrendered to Spirit, one is no longer addicted to that great list of addictive behaviors, and one is no longer compulsively attached to numbing one's pain. When one has an open and dedicated heart and is able to practice non-dual wisdom, and unbearable compassion for Self/self and others, then one is ready to graduate from psychotherapy. At this point one no longer needs to justify one's Being/existence. One simply is at ONE with life and light. This is the beginning of the practice of "conscious dying", which the Lama says is the ultimate practice of Tantra Yoga. Transactional Analysis teaches one to clarify Ego States, purify negative thought processes, love oneself and others and practice win/win relationships throughout life, so one can approach death with equanimity. The Lama Yeshe's offering of Buddha's teachings are much the same as the Corrective Parenting's teaching with the addition of "how to" die consciously. Since we live in a "fast-food" fast-everything culture, we are always looking to reach our goals fast. The Lama Yeshe indicates that the Tantric path on the Middle Way, will bring one to Self faster than the Sutra path will. However, one has to be very fully and totally committed to reaching that level of consciousness. The same is true of reaching "a happy childhood." It takes as long as one doubts and dawdles. One can use a bulldozer, or a demitasse spoon to Renounce the old paradigm on our own personal path. With the coming in of the new love/compassion-based paradigm, and the ensuing chaos as one experiences the changes which are upon us, we find a blending of these two approaches to "reality" and therefore to Self/soul, and rewarding experience.

As the fletcher whittles and makes straight

His arrows, so the master directs his straying

thoughts. Buddha

REFERENCES:

Adler, A. (1932) The Practice and Theory of Individual Psychology. New York. Harcourt Brace and Company

Berne, Eric: (1973) What do you say after you say Hello? Grove Press. New York.

Berne, Eric: (1961) Transactional Analysis and Psychotherapy. Castle Books. New York.

Brook, K.A. (1996) A Fresh look at Permission. Transactional Analysis Journal Vol. 26, No 2. April 1996

Boyd, H.S. (1980) The Structure and Sequence of Psychotherapy. Transactional Analysis Journal. 6. 180-183

Boyd, H.S. and Cowles-Boyd L. (1980) Blocking Tragic Scripts. Transactional Analysis Journal. 10. 227-229

Capra, Frijtov: (1996) The Web of Life. Bantam Books. New York. 1996.

Cassius, J. : (1980) Bodyscripts. Mimeograph copy.

Chamberlain, David: (1988). Babies Remember their Birth. Ballentine Books. New York.

Childs-Gowell, Elaine: (1988). Stages of Ages. Self published.

Childs-Gowell, Elaine: (1979) Reparenting Schizophrenics: The Cathexis Experience. Christopher House. Quincy.Ma. (Now available on-line from I-Universe.com)

Clarke, Jean and Dawson, Connie: (1989) Growing Up Again. Harper Row. San Francisco.

Crossman. P. (1996) Permission and Protection. Transactional Analysis Journal. 114. 139-146

D'Aquili E. Laughlin, C. and McManus J: (1979) The Spectrum of Ritual: A Biogenetic Structural Analysis. Columbia University Press. New York.

De Chardin, Teilhard: (1965) The Phenomenon of Man. New York. Harper Torchbooks.

Eliade. M. (1969) The Quest: History and Meaning in Religion. Chicago. University of Chicago Press.

Emerson. W. (1992-1996) Pre and Perinatal Workshops Seattle and San Francisco

Emerson, W.: with Lynn, S. Lynn, D & Lynn. M.: (1999) Remembering our Home. Paulist Press. California.

Erickson. M. (1980) The Collected Papers of Milton H. Erickson on Hypnosis. (E.L. Rossi ed.) New York. Irvington Press.

Experiencing Enough Workshops Staff (1979-1991). Curriculum and Workshop Processes . Seattle and San Francisco.

Ferguson, Marilyn: (1973) The Brain Revolution. (1973) New York. Taplinger

Gabriel, Michael: (1992). Voices from the Womb. Aslan Publishing. Lower Lake. Ca.

Garcia, Felipe: Reactivity.(1986) Transactional Analysis Journal. Vol 12:2. 123-126

Goulding, M.M and R.L.: (1979) Changing Lives Through Redicision Therapy. New York. Bruner Mazel

Grof, S. (1985) Beyond the Brain: Birth Death and Transcendence in Psychotherapy. Albany New York. State University of New York Press.

Grof, S with Bennet H. (1990) The Holotropic Mind. San Francisco. Harper-Collins.

Grof, S. (1998) The Cosmic Game. New York State University of New York.

Holloway . W (1973) Shut the Escape Hatch. Midwest Institute for Human Understanding. Pp15-118

James M.: (1981) Breaking Free: Breaking Free for a New Life. Reading. Ma. Addison-Wesley.

James, M.: (1974-1978). Workshop Information at ITAA Conferences. San Francisco. Ca.

Janov, Arthur: Imprints: The Lifelong Effects of the Birth Experience. (1983) Coward McCann. New York.

Kuhn, Thomas: (1962) The Structure of Scientific Revolutions. Chicago: University of Chicago Press.

Land, George: (1984) Grow or Die: The Unifying Principle of Transformation. New York. John Wiley & Sons

Landsman, Sandra: (1984) Found A place for Me. Treehouse Enterprises. Farmington Hills. Mi. 1984

Levin, Pamela: (1985) Becoming the Way We Are. Directed Media. Wenatchee. Wa. 1985.

Levin. P. (1989) Cycles of Power: A users guide to the seven seasons of life. Deerfield Beach Fl. Health Communications.

Levine, Peter: (1997) Waking the Tiger. North Atlantic Books. Berkeley. Ca.

Lowen, A. (1980) Bioenergetics. New York. Lancer books

Lucas, W. (1995) Regression Therapy: A Handbook for Professionals: vols I&II Illinois. Deep Forest Press.

Marcher, Elizabeth. (1996) Personal Communication on Rebirth Rituals and Somatic reprocessessing.

Mellor, K: (1975a): Discounting. Transactional Analysis Journa.l 3. 295-203

Mellor, K.: Redefining. Transactional Analysis Journal. 3. 303-311

Moreno, J. (1959) Psychodrama in Arieti: Handbook of Psychiatry II. New York. 1375-1376

Mothersole. Geoff (1996). Existential Realities and No-Suicide Contracts. Transactional Analysis Journal. XXIV (2) 151-159

Peplau, Hildegarde: (1964) Workshop on psychiatry for nurses, lectures and clinical experienced based on Harry Stack Sullivan principles. Chicago. Il.

Perls, F. (1969) Gestalt Therapy Verbatim. New York. Bantam

Prigogine, Ilya, and Stengers: Order out of Chaos: Man's Dialog with Nature. 1983 New York, Bantam.

Reich, W.: (1972) Character Analysis. New York. Simon Shuster.

Schaeffer, B.: Corrective Parenting Chart. Wisconsin. Self Published.

Schiff, Jacqui et al: Cathexis Reader. Transactional Analysis Treatment of Psychosis. Harper and 1975 Row. New York, New York.

Schiff, J. and Schiff, A. (1971) Passivity. Transactional Analysis Journal (1) pp71- 78

Steiner, C. (1971) The Stroke Economy. Transactional Analysis Journal (3) pp9-15

Sullivan, H.S. (1958) The Interpersonal Theory of Psychiatry. New York, W.W. Norton

Tart, Charles: (1975) States of Consciousness. New York. E.P.Dutton.

Thich Nhat Hanh: (1991) Living Buddha, Living Christ. Parallax Press. Berkeley. Ca

Van der Hart. O. (1978) Rituals in Psychotherapy. Irvington Pubs. New York.

Villoldo, Alberfto: (1988) Workshop Information and Four Winds Shamanism. Peru. S. America.

Weinhold, J.A. and Weinhold B. :(1992). Counterdependency the Flight from Intimacy. CIRCL Press. Colorado Springs.

Weiss, L. and Weiss, J. : (1988) Recovery From Codependency. Health communications. Deerfield Beach. Fl.

Yeshe, Lama: (1982) Wisdom Energy. Wisdom Publications. Boston.

Yeshe, Lama (1987) Introduction to Tantra: A Vision of Totality. Wisdom Pubs Boston.

CONTRIBUTORS:

Contributors to the Corrective Parenting Frame-of-Reference and work are in alphabetical order: Kathie Arcide CCP, Lenore Bayuk M.A., ARNP, Sara Lee Blum MA, ARNP, Joan Casey MSW, Kate Casey MA, Elaine Childs Gowell PhD, ARNP, Lee Ford PhD, Sandy Landsman PhD, Pam Levin, Gillian Marrah,MSW, Gail and Harold Nordeman, Wendy Pomeroy PhD, Karuna Poole MA ARNP, John Rhinhart MD, JacquiSchiff and Staff, and countless clients over a period of 26 years who helped develop the Rituals and the Standards of Practice to support the Rituals. Many thanks. These Standards have been developed by a group of Corrective Parent therapists and their clients and while it represents the work of most Corrective Parenting therapists, it does not represent all of them and there are individual variations in style of practice. The most recent revisions are by this author.

ABOUT ELAINE CHILDS GOWELL:

Elaine is a Psychiatric Nurse Practitioner with a private practice in Seattle, Wa. She has practiced since 1970, and was the first Psychiatric Nurse Practitioner to establish a practice in the Northwest. With her husband, Richard Gowell she raised four adopted children who were attachment disordered before this diagnostic category was established. She wishes she had known what she does now in raising their own adopted children. In her practice with adults she recognized that most of her clients had bonding difficulties she called them her"motherless children" because the nature of their discomfort and dysfunction was classically due to lack of attachment and bonding when they were young. Typically her clients' Self Care skills were minimal, many suffer with addictive behaviors and depression, which is often indicative of deep grief. She is certified in a number of modalities including Transactional Analysis, EMDR, Hypnotherapy, EFT, TFT, Cognitive Behavioral processes and Reiki. The Corrective Parenting, Rechilding and Reparenting procedures and "rituals" were developed as a result of Elaine's experience writing her PhD dissertation about the Cathexis Institute in Oakland California where the Reparenting process was developed and her own experience with helping clients heal their developmental needs.She is the author of Reparenting Schizophrenics: the Cathexis Experience. Bodyscript Blockbusting, and Good Grief Rituals. Stages of Ages: it's never too late to have a happy childhood and Regression and Protection: a Handbook for practitioners doing deep regressive work with clients. She teaches workshops and gives speeches on the Good Grief Rituals processes at conferences around the world and continues a private practice in Seattle. Her website is www.goodgriefrituals.com You can learn more about her on this beautiful website.

23863330R00112

Printed in Great Britain
by Amazon